UNITED METHODIST
MEMBERSHIP
RECORD BOOK

of_____
THE UNITED METHODIST CHURCH

at_____

_____District_____Conference

From_____To_____

Prepared and edited by the General Council on Finance and
Administration. Published by the United Methodist Publishing House,
Nashville, Tennessee.

ISBN 978-0687-359134

CONTENTS

PASTOR HISTORY

NAME	DATE OF SERVICE	NAME	DATE OF SERVICE

RECORD OF BAPTISMS
(Recommended)

This record is to report all baptisms administered in the parish.

Each person should be entered chronologically. The baptized person should be posted on the Permanent Church Register, and the chronological number from the register should then be posted on the Record of Baptisms.

The date of baptism and name of the officiating pastor should be entered in the proper column.

Place of birth should include city, county (borough, etc.), state or appropriate geographical or civil divisions for countries outside the United States. List these and the name of the church for the place of baptism.

When the baptized child lives in a community not served by the pastor who administers the Sacrament of Baptism, the pastor is responsible for reporting the baptism to a pastor who serves in the area where the baptized child lives in order that the child may be transferred and the child's name may be entered on the Permanent Church Register of a church in that community (¶233).

When listing parents' names, the inclusion of the mother's maiden name is helpful for historical and familial purposes.

Prepared and edited by the General Council on Finance and Administration. Published by The United Methodist Publishing House, Nashville, Tennessee.

RECORD OF BAPTISMS

Chronological Number	PERSON BAPTIZED	PARENTS/GUARDIANS/SPONSORS/GODPARENTS
	NAME—FAMILY, FIRST, MIDDLE	PARENTS OR GUARDIANS—NAME(S)
	ADDRESS	ADDRESS/
	DATE OF BIRTH / BIRTHPLACE	SPONSORS OR GODPARENTS—NAME(S)
	DATE OF BAPTISM / PLACE OF BAPTISM	ADDRESS
	OFFICIATING PASTOR	ADDITIONAL INFORMATION
	NAME—FAMILY, FIRST, MIDDLE	PARENTS OR GUARDIANS—NAME(S)
	ADDRESS	ADDRESS
	DATE OF BIRTH / BIRTHPLACE	SPONSORS OR GODPARENTS—NAME(S)
	DATE OF BAPTISM / PLACE OF BAPTISM	ADDRESS
	OFFICIATING PASTOR	ADDITIONAL INFORMATION
	NAME—FAMILY, FIRST, MIDDLE	PARENTS OR GUARDIANS—NAME(S)
	ADDRESS	ADDRESS
	DATE OF BIRTH / BIRTHPLACE	SPONSORS OR GODPARENTS—NAME(S)
	DATE OF BAPTISM / PLACE OF BAPTISM	ADDRESS
	OFFICIATING PASTOR	ADDITIONAL INFORMATION
	NAME—FAMILY, FIRST, MIDDLE	PARENTS OR GUARDIANS—NAME(S)
	ADDRESS	ADDRESS
	DATE OF BIRTH / BIRTHPLACE	SPONSORS OR GODPARENTS—NAME(S)
	DATE OF BAPTISM / PLACE OF BAPTISM	ADDRESS/
	OFFICIATING PASTOR	ADDITIONAL INFORMATION

RECORD OF BAPTISMS

Chronological Number	PERSON BAPTIZED			PARENTS/GUARDIANS/SPONSORS/GODPARENTS
	NAME—FAMILY, FIRST, MIDDLE			PARENTS OR GUARDIANS—NAME(S)
	ADDRESS			ADDRESS/
	DATE OF BIRTH	BIRTHPLACE		SPONSORS OR GODPARENTS—NAME(S)
	DATE OF BAPTISM	PLACE OF BAPTISM		ADDRESS
	OFFICIATING PASTOR			ADDITIONAL INFORMATION
	NAME—FAMILY, FIRST, MIDDLE			PARENTS OR GUARDIANS—NAME(S)
	ADDRESS			ADDRESS
	DATE OF BIRTH	BIRTHPLACE		SPONSORS OR GODPARENTS—NAME(S)
	DATE OF BAPTISM	PLACE OF BAPTISM		ADDRESS
	OFFICIATING PASTOR			ADDITIONAL INFORMATION
	NAME—FAMILY, FIRST, MIDDLE			PARENTS OR GUARDIANS—NAME(S)
	ADDRESS			ADDRESS
	DATE OF BIRTH	BIRTHPLACE		SPONSORS OR GODPARENTS—NAME(S)
	DATE OF BAPTISM	PLACE OF BAPTISM		ADDRESS
	OFFICIATING PASTOR			ADDITIONAL INFORMATION
	NAME—FAMILY, FIRST, MIDDLE			PARENTS OR GUARDIANS—NAME(S)
	ADDRESS			ADDRESS
	DATE OF BIRTH	BIRTHPLACE		SPONSORS OR GODPARENTS—NAME(S)
	DATE OF BAPTISM	PLACE OF BAPTISM		ADDRESS/
	OFFICIATING PASTOR			ADDITIONAL INFORMATION

RECORD OF BAPTISMS

Chronological Number	PERSON BAPTIZED			PARENTS/GUARDIANS/SPONSORS/GODPARENTS
	NAME—FAMILY, FIRST, MIDDLE			PARENTS OR GUARDIANS—NAME(S)
	ADDRESS			ADDRESS/
	DATE OF BIRTH	BIRTHPLACE		SPONSORS OR GODPARENTS—NAME(S)
	DATE OF BAPTISM	PLACE OF BAPTISM		ADDRESS
	OFFICIATING PASTOR			ADDITIONAL INFORMATION
	NAME—FAMILY, FIRST, MIDDLE			PARENTS OR GUARDIANS—NAME(S)
	ADDRESS			ADDRESS
	DATE OF BIRTH	BIRTHPLACE		SPONSORS OR GODPARENTS—NAME(S)
	DATE OF BAPTISM	PLACE OF BAPTISM		ADDRESS
	OFFICIATING PASTOR			ADDITIONAL INFORMATION
	NAME—FAMILY, FIRST, MIDDLE			PARENTS OR GUARDIANS—NAME(S)
	ADDRESS			ADDRESS
	DATE OF BIRTH	BIRTHPLACE		SPONSORS OR GODPARENTS—NAME(S)
	DATE OF BAPTISM	PLACE OF BAPTISM		ADDRESS
	OFFICIATING PASTOR			ADDITIONAL INFORMATION
	NAME—FAMILY, FIRST, MIDDLE			PARENTS OR GUARDIANS—NAME(S)
	ADDRESS			ADDRESS
	DATE OF BIRTH	BIRTHPLACE		SPONSORS OR GODPARENTS—NAME(S)
	DATE OF BAPTISM	PLACE OF BAPTISM		ADDRESS/
	OFFICIATING PASTOR			ADDITIONAL INFORMATION

RECORD OF BAPTISMS

Chronological Number	PERSON BAPTIZED	PARENTS/GUARDIANS/SPONSORS/GODPARENTS
	NAME—FAMILY, FIRST, MIDDLE	PARENTS OR GUARDIANS—NAME(S)
	ADDRESS	ADDRESS/
	DATE OF BIRTH / BIRTHPLACE	SPONSORS OR GODPARENTS—NAME(S)
	DATE OF BAPTISM / PLACE OF BAPTISM	ADDRESS
	OFFICIATING PASTOR	ADDITIONAL INFORMATION
	NAME—FAMILY, FIRST, MIDDLE	PARENTS OR GUARDIANS—NAME(S)
	ADDRESS	ADDRESS
	DATE OF BIRTH / BIRTHPLACE	SPONSORS OR GODPARENTS—NAME(S)
	DATE OF BAPTISM / PLACE OF BAPTISM	ADDRESS
	OFFICIATING PASTOR	ADDITIONAL INFORMATION
	NAME—FAMILY, FIRST, MIDDLE	PARENTS OR GUARDIANS—NAME(S)
	ADDRESS	ADDRESS
	DATE OF BIRTH / BIRTHPLACE	SPONSORS OR GODPARENTS—NAME(S)
	DATE OF BAPTISM / PLACE OF BAPTISM	ADDRESS
	OFFICIATING PASTOR	ADDITIONAL INFORMATION
	NAME—FAMILY, FIRST, MIDDLE	PARENTS OR GUARDIANS—NAME(S)
	ADDRESS	ADDRESS
	DATE OF BIRTH / BIRTHPLACE	SPONSORS OR GODPARENTS—NAME(S)
	DATE OF BAPTISM / PLACE OF BAPTISM	ADDRESS/
	OFFICIATING PASTOR	ADDITIONAL INFORMATION

RECORD OF BAPTISMS

Chronological Number	PERSON BAPTIZED			PARENTS/GUARDIANS/SPONSORS/GODPARENTS
	NAME—FAMILY, FIRST, MIDDLE			PARENTS OR GUARDIANS—NAME(S)
	ADDRESS			ADDRESS/
	DATE OF BIRTH	BIRTHPLACE		SPONSORS OR GODPARENTS—NAME(S)
	DATE OF BAPTISM	PLACE OF BAPTISM		ADDRESS
	OFFICIATING PASTOR			ADDITIONAL INFORMATION
	NAME—FAMILY, FIRST, MIDDLE			PARENTS OR GUARDIANS—NAME(S)
	ADDRESS			ADDRESS
	DATE OF BIRTH	BIRTHPLACE		SPONSORS OR GODPARENTS—NAME(S)
	DATE OF BAPTISM	PLACE OF BAPTISM		ADDRESS
	OFFICIATING PASTOR			ADDITIONAL INFORMATION
	NAME—FAMILY, FIRST, MIDDLE			PARENTS OR GUARDIANS—NAME(S)
	ADDRESS			ADDRESS
	DATE OF BIRTH	BIRTHPLACE		SPONSORS OR GODPARENTS—NAME(S)
	DATE OF BAPTISM	PLACE OF BAPTISM		ADDRESS
	OFFICIATING PASTOR			ADDITIONAL INFORMATION
	NAME—FAMILY, FIRST, MIDDLE			PARENTS OR GUARDIANS—NAME(S)
	ADDRESS			ADDRESS
	DATE OF BIRTH	BIRTHPLACE		SPONSORS OR GODPARENTS—NAME(S)
	DATE OF BAPTISM	PLACE OF BAPTISM		ADDRESS/
	OFFICIATING PASTOR			ADDITIONAL INFORMATION

RECORD OF BAPTISMS

Chronological Number	PERSON BAPTIZED	PARENTS/GUARDIANS/SPONSORS/GODPARENTS
	NAME—FAMILY, FIRST, MIDDLE	PARENTS OR GUARDIANS—NAME(S)
	ADDRESS	ADDRESS/
	DATE OF BIRTH / BIRTHPLACE	SPONSORS OR GODPARENTS—NAME(S)
	DATE OF BAPTISM / PLACE OF BAPTISM	ADDRESS
	OFFICIATING PASTOR	ADDITIONAL INFORMATION
	NAME—FAMILY, FIRST, MIDDLE	PARENTS OR GUARDIANS—NAME(S)
	ADDRESS	ADDRESS
	DATE OF BIRTH / BIRTHPLACE	SPONSORS OR GODPARENTS—NAME(S)
	DATE OF BAPTISM / PLACE OF BAPTISM	ADDRESS
	OFFICIATING PASTOR	ADDITIONAL INFORMATION
	NAME—FAMILY, FIRST, MIDDLE	PARENTS OR GUARDIANS—NAME(S)
	ADDRESS	ADDRESS
	DATE OF BIRTH / BIRTHPLACE	SPONSORS OR GODPARENTS—NAME(S)
	DATE OF BAPTISM / PLACE OF BAPTISM	ADDRESS
	OFFICIATING PASTOR	ADDITIONAL INFORMATION
	NAME—FAMILY, FIRST, MIDDLE	PARENTS OR GUARDIANS—NAME(S)
	ADDRESS	ADDRESS
	DATE OF BIRTH / BIRTHPLACE	SPONSORS OR GODPARENTS—NAME(S)
	DATE OF BAPTISM / PLACE OF BAPTISM	ADDRESS/
	OFFICIATING PASTOR	ADDITIONAL INFORMATION

RECORD OF BAPTISMS

Chronological Number	PERSON BAPTIZED	PARENTS/GUARDIANS/SPONSORS/GODPARENTS
	NAME—FAMILY, FIRST, MIDDLE	PARENTS OR GUARDIANS—NAME(S)
	ADDRESS	ADDRESS/
	DATE OF BIRTH — BIRTHPLACE	SPONSORS OR GODPARENTS—NAME(S)
	DATE OF BAPTISM — PLACE OF BAPTISM	ADDRESS
	OFFICIATING PASTOR	ADDITIONAL INFORMATION
	NAME—FAMILY, FIRST, MIDDLE	PARENTS OR GUARDIANS—NAME(S)
	ADDRESS	ADDRESS
	DATE OF BIRTH — BIRTHPLACE	SPONSORS OR GODPARENTS—NAME(S)
	DATE OF BAPTISM — PLACE OF BAPTISM	ADDRESS
	OFFICIATING PASTOR	ADDITIONAL INFORMATION
	NAME—FAMILY, FIRST, MIDDLE	PARENTS OR GUARDIANS—NAME(S)
	ADDRESS	ADDRESS
	DATE OF BIRTH — BIRTHPLACE	SPONSORS OR GODPARENTS—NAME(S)
	DATE OF BAPTISM — PLACE OF BAPTISM	ADDRESS
	OFFICIATING PASTOR	ADDITIONAL INFORMATION
	NAME—FAMILY, FIRST, MIDDLE	PARENTS OR GUARDIANS—NAME(S)
	ADDRESS	ADDRESS
	DATE OF BIRTH — BIRTHPLACE	SPONSORS OR GODPARENTS—NAME(S)
	DATE OF BAPTISM — PLACE OF BAPTISM	ADDRESS/
	OFFICIATING PASTOR	ADDITIONAL INFORMATION

RECORD OF BAPTISMS

Chronological Number	PERSON BAPTIZED	PARENTS/GUARDIANS/SPONSORS/GODPARENTS
	NAME—FAMILY, FIRST, MIDDLE	PARENTS OR GUARDIANS—NAME(S)
	ADDRESS	ADDRESS/
	DATE OF BIRTH / BIRTHPLACE	SPONSORS OR GODPARENTS—NAME(S)
	DATE OF BAPTISM / PLACE OF BAPTISM	ADDRESS
	OFFICIATING PASTOR	ADDITIONAL INFORMATION
	NAME—FAMILY, FIRST, MIDDLE	PARENTS OR GUARDIANS—NAME(S)
	ADDRESS	ADDRESS
	DATE OF BIRTH / BIRTHPLACE	SPONSORS OR GODPARENTS—NAME(S)
	DATE OF BAPTISM / PLACE OF BAPTISM	ADDRESS
	OFFICIATING PASTOR	ADDITIONAL INFORMATION
	NAME—FAMILY, FIRST, MIDDLE	PARENTS OR GUARDIANS—NAME(S)
	ADDRESS	ADDRESS
	DATE OF BIRTH / BIRTHPLACE	SPONSORS OR GODPARENTS—NAME(S)
	DATE OF BAPTISM / PLACE OF BAPTISM	ADDRESS
	OFFICIATING PASTOR	ADDITIONAL INFORMATION
	NAME—FAMILY, FIRST, MIDDLE	PARENTS OR GUARDIANS—NAME(S)
	ADDRESS	ADDRESS
	DATE OF BIRTH / BIRTHPLACE	SPONSORS OR GODPARENTS—NAME(S)
	DATE OF BAPTISM / PLACE OF BAPTISM	ADDRESS/
	OFFICIATING PASTOR	ADDITIONAL INFORMATION

RECORD OF BAPTISMS

Chronological Number	PERSON BAPTIZED			PARENTS/GUARDIANS/SPONSORS/GODPARENTS
	NAME—FAMILY, FIRST, MIDDLE			PARENTS OR GUARDIANS—NAME(S)
	ADDRESS			ADDRESS/
	DATE OF BIRTH	BIRTHPLACE		SPONSORS OR GODPARENTS—NAME(S)
	DATE OF BAPTISM	PLACE OF BAPTISM		ADDRESS
	OFFICIATING PASTOR			ADDITIONAL INFORMATION
	NAME—FAMILY, FIRST, MIDDLE			PARENTS OR GUARDIANS—NAME(S)
	ADDRESS			ADDRESS
	DATE OF BIRTH	BIRTHPLACE		SPONSORS OR GODPARENTS—NAME(S)
	DATE OF BAPTISM	PLACE OF BAPTISM		ADDRESS
	OFFICIATING PASTOR			ADDITIONAL INFORMATION
	NAME—FAMILY, FIRST, MIDDLE			PARENTS OR GUARDIANS—NAME(S)
	ADDRESS			ADDRESS
	DATE OF BIRTH	BIRTHPLACE		SPONSORS OR GODPARENTS—NAME(S)
	DATE OF BAPTISM	PLACE OF BAPTISM		ADDRESS
	OFFICIATING PASTOR			ADDITIONAL INFORMATION
	NAME—FAMILY, FIRST, MIDDLE			PARENTS OR GUARDIANS—NAME(S)
	ADDRESS			ADDRESS
	DATE OF BIRTH	BIRTHPLACE		SPONSORS OR GODPARENTS—NAME(S)
	DATE OF BAPTISM	PLACE OF BAPTISM		ADDRESS/
	OFFICIATING PASTOR			ADDITIONAL INFORMATION

RECORD OF BAPTISMS

Chronological Number	PERSON BAPTIZED			PARENTS/GUARDIANS/SPONSORS/GODPARENTS
	NAME—FAMILY, FIRST, MIDDLE			PARENTS OR GUARDIANS—NAME(S)
	ADDRESS			ADDRESS/
	DATE OF BIRTH	BIRTHPLACE		SPONSORS OR GODPARENTS—NAME(S)
	DATE OF BAPTISM	PLACE OF BAPTISM		ADDRESS
	OFFICIATING PASTOR			ADDITIONAL INFORMATION
	NAME—FAMILY, FIRST, MIDDLE			PARENTS OR GUARDIANS—NAME(S)
	ADDRESS			ADDRESS
	DATE OF BIRTH	BIRTHPLACE		SPONSORS OR GODPARENTS—NAME(S)
	DATE OF BAPTISM	PLACE OF BAPTISM		ADDRESS
	OFFICIATING PASTOR			ADDITIONAL INFORMATION
	NAME—FAMILY, FIRST, MIDDLE			PARENTS OR GUARDIANS—NAME(S)
	ADDRESS			ADDRESS
	DATE OF BIRTH	BIRTHPLACE		SPONSORS OR GODPARENTS—NAME(S)
	DATE OF BAPTISM	PLACE OF BAPTISM		ADDRESS
	OFFICIATING PASTOR			ADDITIONAL INFORMATION
	NAME—FAMILY, FIRST, MIDDLE			PARENTS OR GUARDIANS—NAME(S)
	ADDRESS			ADDRESS
	DATE OF BIRTH	BIRTHPLACE		SPONSORS OR GODPARENTS—NAME(S)
	DATE OF BAPTISM	PLACE OF BAPTISM		ADDRESS/
	OFFICIATING PASTOR			ADDITIONAL INFORMATION

RECORD OF BAPTISMS

Chronological Number	PERSON BAPTIZED			PARENTS/GUARDIANS/SPONSORS/GODPARENTS
	NAME—FAMILY, FIRST, MIDDLE			PARENTS OR GUARDIANS—NAME(S)
	ADDRESS			ADDRESS/
	DATE OF BIRTH	BIRTHPLACE		SPONSORS OR GODPARENTS—NAME(S)
	DATE OF BAPTISM		PLACE OF BAPTISM	ADDRESS
	OFFICIATING PASTOR			ADDITIONAL INFORMATION
	NAME—FAMILY, FIRST, MIDDLE			PARENTS OR GUARDIANS—NAME(S)
	ADDRESS			ADDRESS
	DATE OF BIRTH	BIRTHPLACE		SPONSORS OR GODPARENTS—NAME(S)
	DATE OF BAPTISM		PLACE OF BAPTISM	ADDRESS
	OFFICIATING PASTOR			ADDITIONAL INFORMATION
	NAME—FAMILY, FIRST, MIDDLE			PARENTS OR GUARDIANS—NAME(S)
	ADDRESS			ADDRESS
	DATE OF BIRTH	BIRTHPLACE		SPONSORS OR GODPARENTS—NAME(S)
	DATE OF BAPTISM		PLACE OF BAPTISM	ADDRESS
	OFFICIATING PASTOR			ADDITIONAL INFORMATION
	NAME—FAMILY, FIRST, MIDDLE			PARENTS OR GUARDIANS—NAME(S)
	ADDRESS			ADDRESS
	DATE OF BIRTH	BIRTHPLACE		SPONSORS OR GODPARENTS—NAME(S)
	DATE OF BAPTISM		PLACE OF BAPTISM	ADDRESS/
	OFFICIATING PASTOR			ADDITIONAL INFORMATION

RECORD OF BAPTISMS

Chronological Number	PERSON BAPTIZED			PARENTS/GUARDIANS/SPONSORS/GODPARENTS
	NAME—FAMILY, FIRST, MIDDLE			PARENTS OR GUARDIANS—NAME(S)
	ADDRESS			ADDRESS/
	DATE OF BIRTH	BIRTHPLACE		SPONSORS OR GODPARENTS—NAME(S)
	DATE OF BAPTISM	PLACE OF BAPTISM		ADDRESS
	OFFICIATING PASTOR			ADDITIONAL INFORMATION
	NAME—FAMILY, FIRST, MIDDLE			PARENTS OR GUARDIANS—NAME(S)
	ADDRESS			ADDRESS
	DATE OF BIRTH	BIRTHPLACE		SPONSORS OR GODPARENTS—NAME(S)
	DATE OF BAPTISM	PLACE OF BAPTISM		ADDRESS
	OFFICIATING PASTOR			ADDITIONAL INFORMATION
	NAME—FAMILY, FIRST, MIDDLE			PARENTS OR GUARDIANS—NAME(S)
	ADDRESS			ADDRESS
	DATE OF BIRTH	BIRTHPLACE		SPONSORS OR GODPARENTS—NAME(S)
	DATE OF BAPTISM	PLACE OF BAPTISM		ADDRESS
	OFFICIATING PASTOR			ADDITIONAL INFORMATION
	NAME—FAMILY, FIRST, MIDDLE			PARENTS OR GUARDIANS—NAME(S)
	ADDRESS			ADDRESS
	DATE OF BIRTH	BIRTHPLACE		SPONSORS OR GODPARENTS—NAME(S)
	DATE OF BAPTISM	PLACE OF BAPTISM		ADDRESS/
	OFFICIATING PASTOR			ADDITIONAL INFORMATION

RECORD OF BAPTISMS

Chronological Number	PERSON BAPTIZED			PARENTS/GUARDIANS/SPONSORS/GODPARENTS	
	NAME—FAMILY, FIRST, MIDDLE			PARENTS OR GUARDIANS—NAME(S)	
	ADDRESS			ADDRESS/	
	DATE OF BIRTH	BIRTHPLACE		SPONSORS OR GODPARENTS—NAME(S)	
	DATE OF BAPTISM	PLACE OF BAPTISM		ADDRESS	
	OFFICIATING PASTOR			ADDITIONAL INFORMATION	
	NAME—FAMILY, FIRST, MIDDLE			PARENTS OR GUARDIANS—NAME(S)	
	ADDRESS			ADDRESS	
	DATE OF BIRTH	BIRTHPLACE		SPONSORS OR GODPARENTS—NAME(S)	
	DATE OF BAPTISM	PLACE OF BAPTISM		ADDRESS	
	OFFICIATING PASTOR			ADDITIONAL INFORMATION	
	NAME—FAMILY, FIRST, MIDDLE			PARENTS OR GUARDIANS—NAME(S)	
	ADDRESS			ADDRESS	
	DATE OF BIRTH	BIRTHPLACE		SPONSORS OR GODPARENTS—NAME(S)	
	DATE OF BAPTISM	PLACE OF BAPTISM		ADDRESS	
	OFFICIATING PASTOR			ADDITIONAL INFORMATION	
	NAME—FAMILY, FIRST, MIDDLE			PARENTS OR GUARDIANS—NAME(S)	
	ADDRESS			ADDRESS	
	DATE OF BIRTH	BIRTHPLACE		SPONSORS OR GODPARENTS—NAME(S)	
	DATE OF BAPTISM	PLACE OF BAPTISM		ADDRESS/	
	OFFICIATING PASTOR			ADDITIONAL INFORMATION	

RECORD OF BAPTISMS

Chronological Number	PERSON BAPTIZED			PARENTS/GUARDIANS/SPONSORS/GODPARENTS
	NAME—FAMILY, FIRST, MIDDLE			PARENTS OR GUARDIANS—NAME(S)
	ADDRESS			ADDRESS/
	DATE OF BIRTH	BIRTHPLACE		SPONSORS OR GODPARENTS—NAME(S)
	DATE OF BAPTISM	PLACE OF BAPTISM		ADDRESS
	OFFICIATING PASTOR			ADDITIONAL INFORMATION
	NAME—FAMILY, FIRST, MIDDLE			PARENTS OR GUARDIANS—NAME(S)
	ADDRESS			ADDRESS
	DATE OF BIRTH	BIRTHPLACE		SPONSORS OR GODPARENTS—NAME(S)
	DATE OF BAPTISM	PLACE OF BAPTISM		ADDRESS
	OFFICIATING PASTOR			ADDITIONAL INFORMATION
	NAME—FAMILY, FIRST, MIDDLE			PARENTS OR GUARDIANS—NAME(S)
	ADDRESS			ADDRESS
	DATE OF BIRTH	BIRTHPLACE		SPONSORS OR GODPARENTS—NAME(S)
	DATE OF BAPTISM	PLACE OF BAPTISM		ADDRESS
	OFFICIATING PASTOR			ADDITIONAL INFORMATION
	NAME—FAMILY, FIRST, MIDDLE			PARENTS OR GUARDIANS—NAME(S)
	ADDRESS			ADDRESS
	DATE OF BIRTH	BIRTHPLACE		SPONSORS OR GODPARENTS—NAME(S)
	DATE OF BAPTISM	PLACE OF BAPTISM		ADDRESS/
	OFFICIATING PASTOR			ADDITIONAL INFORMATION

RECORD OF BAPTISMS

Chronolog ical Number	PERSON BAPTIZED			PARENTS/GUARDIANS/SPONSORS/GODPARENTS
	NAME—FAMILY, FIRST, MIDDLE			PARENTS OR GUARDIANS—NAME(S)
	ADDRESS			ADDRESS/
	DATE OF BIRTH	BIRTHPLACE		SPONSORS OR GODPARENTS—NAME(S)
	DATE OF BAPTISM	PLACE OF BAPTISM		ADDRESS
	OFFICIATING PASTOR			ADDITIONAL INFORMATION
	NAME—FAMILY, FIRST, MIDDLE			PARENTS OR GUARDIANS—NAME(S)
	ADDRESS			ADDRESS
	DATE OF BIRTH	BIRTHPLACE		SPONSORS OR GODPARENTS—NAME(S)
	DATE OF BAPTISM	PLACE OF BAPTISM		ADDRESS
	OFFICIATING PASTOR			ADDITIONAL INFORMATION
	NAME—FAMILY, FIRST, MIDDLE			PARENTS OR GUARDIANS—NAME(S)
	ADDRESS			ADDRESS
	DATE OF BIRTH	BIRTHPLACE		SPONSORS OR GODPARENTS—NAME(S)
	DATE OF BAPTISM	PLACE OF BAPTISM		ADDRESS
	OFFICIATING PASTOR			ADDITIONAL INFORMATION
	NAME—FAMILY, FIRST, MIDDLE			PARENTS OR GUARDIANS—NAME(S)
	ADDRESS			ADDRESS
	DATE OF BIRTH	BIRTHPLACE		SPONSORS OR GODPARENTS—NAME(S)
	DATE OF BAPTISM	PLACE OF BAPTISM		ADDRESS/
	OFFICIATING PASTOR			ADDITIONAL INFORMATION

RECORD OF BAPTISMS

Chronological Number	PERSON BAPTIZED			PARENTS/GUARDIANS/SPONSORS/GODPARENTS
	NAME—FAMILY, FIRST, MIDDLE			PARENTS OR GUARDIANS—NAME(S)
	ADDRESS			ADDRESS/
	DATE OF BIRTH	BIRTHPLACE		SPONSORS OR GODPARENTS—NAME(S)
	DATE OF BAPTISM		PLACE OF BAPTISM	ADDRESS
	OFFICIATING PASTOR			ADDITIONAL INFORMATION
	NAME—FAMILY, FIRST, MIDDLE			PARENTS OR GUARDIANS—NAME(S)
	ADDRESS			ADDRESS
	DATE OF BIRTH	BIRTHPLACE		SPONSORS OR GODPARENTS—NAME(S)
	DATE OF BAPTISM		PLACE OF BAPTISM	ADDRESS
	OFFICIATING PASTOR			ADDITIONAL INFORMATION
	NAME—FAMILY, FIRST, MIDDLE			PARENTS OR GUARDIANS—NAME(S)
	ADDRESS			ADDRESS
	DATE OF BIRTH	BIRTHPLACE		SPONSORS OR GODPARENTS—NAME(S)
	DATE OF BAPTISM		PLACE OF BAPTISM	ADDRESS
	OFFICIATING PASTOR			ADDITIONAL INFORMATION
	NAME—FAMILY, FIRST, MIDDLE			PARENTS OR GUARDIANS—NAME(S)
	ADDRESS			ADDRESS
	DATE OF BIRTH	BIRTHPLACE		SPONSORS OR GODPARENTS—NAME(S)
	DATE OF BAPTISM		PLACE OF BAPTISM	ADDRESS/
	OFFICIATING PASTOR			ADDITIONAL INFORMATION

RECORD OF BAPTISMS

Chronological Number	PERSON BAPTIZED			PARENTS/GUARDIANS/SPONSORS/GODPARENTS
	NAME—FAMILY, FIRST, MIDDLE			PARENTS OR GUARDIANS—NAME(S)
	ADDRESS			ADDRESS/
	DATE OF BIRTH	BIRTHPLACE		SPONSORS OR GODPARENTS—NAME(S)
	DATE OF BAPTISM	PLACE OF BAPTISM		ADDRESS
	OFFICIATING PASTOR			ADDITIONAL INFORMATION
	NAME—FAMILY, FIRST, MIDDLE			PARENTS OR GUARDIANS—NAME(S)
	ADDRESS			ADDRESS
	DATE OF BIRTH	BIRTHPLACE		SPONSORS OR GODPARENTS—NAME(S)
	DATE OF BAPTISM	PLACE OF BAPTISM		ADDRESS
	OFFICIATING PASTOR			ADDITIONAL INFORMATION
	NAME—FAMILY, FIRST, MIDDLE			PARENTS OR GUARDIANS—NAME(S)
	ADDRESS			ADDRESS
	DATE OF BIRTH	BIRTHPLACE		SPONSORS OR GODPARENTS—NAME(S)
	DATE OF BAPTISM	PLACE OF BAPTISM		ADDRESS
	OFFICIATING PASTOR			ADDITIONAL INFORMATION
	NAME—FAMILY, FIRST, MIDDLE			PARENTS OR GUARDIANS—NAME(S)
	ADDRESS			ADDRESS
	DATE OF BIRTH	BIRTHPLACE		SPONSORS OR GODPARENTS—NAME(S)
	DATE OF BAPTISM	PLACE OF BAPTISM		ADDRESS/
	OFFICIATING PASTOR			ADDITIONAL INFORMATION

RECORD OF BAPTISMS

Chronological Number	PERSON BAPTIZED	PARENTS/GUARDIANS/SPONSORS/GODPARENTS
	NAME—FAMILY, FIRST, MIDDLE	PARENTS OR GUARDIANS—NAME(S)
	ADDRESS	ADDRESS/
	DATE OF BIRTH / BIRTHPLACE	SPONSORS OR GODPARENTS—NAME(S)
	DATE OF BAPTISM / PLACE OF BAPTISM	ADDRESS
	OFFICIATING PASTOR	ADDITIONAL INFORMATION
	NAME—FAMILY, FIRST, MIDDLE	PARENTS OR GUARDIANS—NAME(S)
	ADDRESS	ADDRESS
	DATE OF BIRTH / BIRTHPLACE	SPONSORS OR GODPARENTS—NAME(S)
	DATE OF BAPTISM / PLACE OF BAPTISM	ADDRESS
	OFFICIATING PASTOR	ADDITIONAL INFORMATION
	NAME—FAMILY, FIRST, MIDDLE	PARENTS OR GUARDIANS—NAME(S)
	ADDRESS	ADDRESS
	DATE OF BIRTH / BIRTHPLACE	SPONSORS OR GODPARENTS—NAME(S)
	DATE OF BAPTISM / PLACE OF BAPTISM	ADDRESS
	OFFICIATING PASTOR	ADDITIONAL INFORMATION
	NAME—FAMILY, FIRST, MIDDLE	PARENTS OR GUARDIANS—NAME(S)
	ADDRESS	ADDRESS
	DATE OF BIRTH / BIRTHPLACE	SPONSORS OR GODPARENTS—NAME(S)
	DATE OF BAPTISM / PLACE OF BAPTISM	ADDRESS/
	OFFICIATING PASTOR	ADDITIONAL INFORMATION

RECORD OF BAPTISMS

Chronolog ical Number	PERSON BAPTIZED			PARENTS/GUARDIANS/SPONSORS/GODPARENTS	
	NAME—FAMILY, FIRST, MIDDLE			PARENTS OR GUARDIANS—NAME(S)	
	ADDRESS			ADDRESS/	
	DATE OF BIRTH	BIRTHPLACE		SPONSORS OR GODPARENTS—NAME(S)	
	DATE OF BAPTISM	PLACE OF BAPTISM		ADDRESS	
	OFFICIATING PASTOR			ADDITIONAL INFORMATION	
	NAME—FAMILY, FIRST, MIDDLE			PARENTS OR GUARDIANS—NAME(S)	
	ADDRESS			ADDRESS	
	DATE OF BIRTH	BIRTHPLACE		SPONSORS OR GODPARENTS—NAME(S)	
	DATE OF BAPTISM	PLACE OF BAPTISM		ADDRESS	
	OFFICIATING PASTOR			ADDITIONAL INFORMATION	
	NAME—FAMILY, FIRST, MIDDLE			PARENTS OR GUARDIANS—NAME(S)	
	ADDRESS			ADDRESS	
	DATE OF BIRTH	BIRTHPLACE		SPONSORS OR GODPARENTS—NAME(S)	
	DATE OF BAPTISM	PLACE OF BAPTISM		ADDRESS	
	OFFICIATING PASTOR			ADDITIONAL INFORMATION	
	NAME—FAMILY, FIRST, MIDDLE			PARENTS OR GUARDIANS—NAME(S)	
	ADDRESS			ADDRESS	
	DATE OF BIRTH	BIRTHPLACE		SPONSORS OR GODPARENTS—NAME(S)	
	DATE OF BAPTISM	PLACE OF BAPTISM		ADDRESS/	
	OFFICIATING PASTOR			ADDITIONAL INFORMATION	

RECORD OF BAPTISMS

Chronological Number	PERSON BAPTIZED			PARENTS/GUARDIANS/SPONSORS/GODPARENTS
	NAME—FAMILY, FIRST, MIDDLE			PARENTS OR GUARDIANS—NAME(S)
	ADDRESS			ADDRESS/
	DATE OF BIRTH	BIRTHPLACE		SPONSORS OR GODPARENTS—NAME(S)
	DATE OF BAPTISM	PLACE OF BAPTISM		ADDRESS
	OFFICIATING PASTOR			ADDITIONAL INFORMATION
	NAME—FAMILY, FIRST, MIDDLE			PARENTS OR GUARDIANS—NAME(S)
	ADDRESS			ADDRESS
	DATE OF BIRTH	BIRTHPLACE		SPONSORS OR GODPARENTS—NAME(S)
	DATE OF BAPTISM	PLACE OF BAPTISM		ADDRESS
	OFFICIATING PASTOR			ADDITIONAL INFORMATION
	NAME—FAMILY, FIRST, MIDDLE			PARENTS OR GUARDIANS—NAME(S)
	ADDRESS			ADDRESS
	DATE OF BIRTH	BIRTHPLACE		SPONSORS OR GODPARENTS—NAME(S)
	DATE OF BAPTISM	PLACE OF BAPTISM		ADDRESS
	OFFICIATING PASTOR			ADDITIONAL INFORMATION
	NAME—FAMILY, FIRST, MIDDLE			PARENTS OR GUARDIANS—NAME(S)
	ADDRESS			ADDRESS
	DATE OF BIRTH	BIRTHPLACE		SPONSORS OR GODPARENTS—NAME(S)
	DATE OF BAPTISM	PLACE OF BAPTISM		ADDRESS/
	OFFICIATING PASTOR			ADDITIONAL INFORMATION

PERMANENT CHURCH REGISTER
(Formerly known as the Chronological Roll of Full Members)
(Required)

This is the permanent record required by *The Book of Discipline of The United Methodist Church*. Copies should be made of it and kept in a safe place in case of fire or destruction. Since pages can be removed from the post binder, copies can be made.

This membership record should be kept up-to-date and in chronological order. Additional volumes can be added when membership expands. Post extensions are available.

Enter all pertinent information such as full name and date of birth. Under "Received as a Baptized Member," please mark the date of baptism if the member was baptized in the local church or the date the person was received by transfer if applicable. All members on your register should have a date in this column. Under "How" please mark (B) Baptized, T (transfer from another United Methodist church), or OD (from other denominations)..

Under the "Received as Professing Member" column, if applicable, indicate date and how, e.g., PF (profession of Christian faith), R (Restored), T (transfer from another United Methodist church), or OD (from other denominations).

To facilitate the gathering of racial/ethnic data on church members, record in the "Racial/Ethnic" column the appropriate letter from the key on the bottom of the form. To facilitate gathering gender data, record the appropriate letter (F or M) from the key on the bottom of the form in the "Gender" column.

The last four columns for removals help audit each chronological page and provide necessary data for charge and annual conference reports in an easily verifiable way. Under the column "How" the type of action taken may be T (transfer to another UMC), OD (to other denomination), D (death), WD (withdrawal), WC (withdrawal under charges) or CC (charge conference action). In the columns headed "B" (Baptized Member) and "P" (Professing Member), please put a check mark if the person's membership is removed from that category. NOTE THAT BAPTIZED MEMBERS CAN BE REMOVED FROM THE CHURCH REGISTER ONLY THROUGH TRANSFER TO ANOTHER UMC, TRANSFER TO OTHER DENOMINATIONS, OR DEATH. (For instance, if a professing member transfers to another UMC, there would be a check mark in both categories as that member will no longer be a member of this fellowship. If, however, a professing member is removed by charge conference action, there would be a check mark only under professing member, indicating that this person remains on the church register as a baptized member.)

ADDING BAPTIZED MEMBERS TO YOUR PERMANENT CHURCH REGISTER: Starting in 2005, Baptized persons are to be added to the Permanent Church Register as they are now, according to the *Discipline*, members of the local church. It is recommended that, churches begin by adding the baptized persons who were on the previously existing Preparatory Roll as of December 31, 2004. (Note that after January 1, 2005, the Preparatory Roll no longer exists.) It is not necessary to go back historically to add persons to the Register, but do note that all professing members on the Register to date are also baptized members and need to be treated accordingly in regard to membership removals when performing the audits. Beginning with January 1, 2005, all newly received baptized members are to be recorded on this Permanent Church Register.

Prepared and edited by the General Council on Finance and Administration. Published by The United Methodist Publishing House, Nashville, Tennessee.

PERMANENT CHURCH REGISTER

| CHRONO-LOGICAL NUMBER | NAME | | DATE OF BIRTH | RACIAL/ ETHNIC GROUP | GENDER | RECEIVED AS BAPTIZED MEMBER (B) | | | RECEIVED AS PROFESSING MEMBER (P) | | | REMOVED | | B | P |
| | FIRST | MIDDLE | | | | DATE | HOW | | DATE | HOW | | DATE | HOW | | |
	FAMILY														
	CHURCH TRANSFERRED FROM:					CHURCH TRANSFERRED TO:									
	CHURCH TRANSFERRED FROM:					CHURCH TRANSFERRED TO:									
	CHURCH TRANSFERRED FROM:					CHURCH TRANSFERRED TO:									
	CHURCH TRANSFERRED FROM:					CHURCH TRANSFERRED TO:									
	CHURCH TRANSFERRED FROM:					CHURCH TRANSFERRED TO:									
	CHURCH TRANSFERRED FROM:					CHURCH TRANSFERRED TO:									
	CHURCH TRANSFERRED FROM:					CHURCH TRANSFERRED TO:									
	CHURCH TRANSFERRED FROM:					CHURCH TRANSFERRED TO:									
	CHURCH TRANSFERRED FROM:					CHURCH TRANSFERRED TO:									

A-Asian   AA/B-African American/Black   H-Hispanic   N-Native American   P-Pacific Islander   W-White   MR-Multi-Racial   M-Male   F-Female

T-Transfer   OD-Other Denomination   PF-Profession of Christian Faith   R-Restored   CC-Charge Conf. Action   WD-Withdrawal   WC-Withdrawal under Charges   D-Death

27

PERMANENT CHURCH REGISTER

CHRONO-LOGICAL NUMBER	NAME			DATE OF BIRTH	RACIAL/ETHNIC GROUP	GENDER	RECEIVED AS BAPTIZED MEMBER (B)		RECEIVED AS PROFESSING MEMBER (P)			REMOVED		B	P
	FAMILY	FIRST	MIDDLE				DATE	HOW	DATE	HOW		DATE	HOW		
	CHURCH TRANSFERRED FROM:						CHURCH TRANSFERRED TO:								
	CHURCH TRANSFERRED FROM:						CHURCH TRANSFERRED TO:								
	CHURCH TRANSFERRED FROM:						CHURCH TRANSFERRED TO:								
	CHURCH TRANSFERRED FROM:						CHURCH TRANSFERRED TO:								
	CHURCH TRANSFERRED FROM:						CHURCH TRANSFERRED TO:								
	CHURCH TRANSFERRED FROM:						CHURCH TRANSFERRED TO:								
	CHURCH TRANSFERRED FROM:						CHURCH TRANSFERRED TO:								
	CHURCH TRANSFERRED FROM:						CHURCH TRANSFERRED TO:								
	CHURCH TRANSFERRED FROM:						CHURCH TRANSFERRED TO:								

A-Asian   AA/B-African American/Black   H-Hispanic   N-Native American   P-Pacific Islander   W-White   MR-Multi-Racial   F-Female   M-Male
T-Transfer   OD-Other Denomination   PF-Profession of Christian Faith   R-Restored   CC-Charge Conf. Action   WD-Withdrawal   WC-Withdrawal under Charges   D-Death

28

PERMANENT CHURCH REGISTER

CHRONO-LOGICAL NUMBER	NAME		DATE OF BIRTH	RACIAL/ ETHNIC GROUP	GENDER	RECEIVED AS BAPTIZED MEMBER (B)		RECEIVED AS PROFESSING MEMBER (P)		REMOVED		B	P
	FAMILY	FIRST / MIDDLE				DATE	HOW	DATE	HOW	DATE	HOW		
	CHURCH TRANSFERRED FROM:					CHURCH TRANSFERRED TO:							
	CHURCH TRANSFERRED FROM:					CHURCH TRANSFERRED TO:							
	CHURCH TRANSFERRED FROM:					CHURCH TRANSFERRED TO:							
	CHURCH TRANSFERRED FROM:					CHURCH TRANSFERRED TO:							
	CHURCH TRANSFERRED FROM:					CHURCH TRANSFERRED TO:							
	CHURCH TRANSFERRED FROM:					CHURCH TRANSFERRED TO:							
	CHURCH TRANSFERRED FROM:					CHURCH TRANSFERRED TO:							
	CHURCH TRANSFERRED FROM:					CHURCH TRANSFERRED TO:							
	CHURCH TRANSFERRED FROM:					CHURCH TRANSFERRED TO:							

A-Asian   AA/B-African American/Black   H-Hispanic   N-Native American   P-Pacific Islander   W-White   MR-Multi-Racial   F-Female   M-Male

T-Transfer   OD-Other Denomination   PF-Profession of Christian Faith   R-Restored   CC-Charge Conf. Action   WD-Withdrawal   WC-Withdrawal under Charges   D-Death

PERMANENT CHURCH REGISTER

| CHRONO-LOGICAL NUMBER | NAME | | | DATE OF BIRTH | RACIAL/ ETHNIC GROUP | GENDER | RECEIVED AS BAPTIZED MEMBER (B) | | RECEIVED AS PROFESSING MEMBER (P) | | REMOVED | | B | P |
	FAMILY	FIRST	MIDDLE				DATE	HOW	DATE	HOW	DATE	HOW		
	CHURCH TRANSFERRED FROM:							CHURCH TRANSFERRED TO:						
	CHURCH TRANSFERRED FROM:							CHURCH TRANSFERRED TO:						
	CHURCH TRANSFERRED FROM:							CHURCH TRANSFERRED TO:						
	CHURCH TRANSFERRED FROM:							CHURCH TRANSFERRED TO:						
	CHURCH TRANSFERRED FROM:							CHURCH TRANSFERRED TO:						
	CHURCH TRANSFERRED FROM:							CHURCH TRANSFERRED TO:						
	CHURCH TRANSFERRED FROM:							CHURCH TRANSFERRED TO:						
	CHURCH TRANSFERRED FROM:							CHURCH TRANSFERRED TO:						
	CHURCH TRANSFERRED FROM:							CHURCH TRANSFERRED TO:						

A-Asian   AA/B-African American/Black   H-Hispanic   N-Native American   P-Pacific Islander   W-White   MR-Multi-Racial   F-Female   M-Male
T-Transfer   OD-Other Denomination   PF-Profession of Christian Faith   R-Restored   CC-Charge Conf. Action   WD-Withdrawal   WC-Withdrawal under Charges   D-Death

PERMANENT CHURCH REGISTER

CHRONO-LOGICAL NUMBER	NAME			DATE OF BIRTH	RACIAL/ ETHNIC GROUP	GENDER	RECEIVED AS BAPTIZED MEMBER (B)		RECEIVED AS PROFESSING MEMBER (P)		REMOVED		HOW	B	P
	FAMILY	FIRST	MIDDLE				DATE	HOW	DATE	HOW	DATE				
	CHURCH TRANSFERRED FROM:							CHURCH TRANSFERRED TO:							
	CHURCH TRANSFERRED FROM:							CHURCH TRANSFERRED TO:							
	CHURCH TRANSFERRED FROM:							CHURCH TRANSFERRED TO:							
	CHURCH TRANSFERRED FROM:							CHURCH TRANSFERRED TO:							
	CHURCH TRANSFERRED FROM:							CHURCH TRANSFERRED TO:							
	CHURCH TRANSFERRED FROM:							CHURCH TRANSFERRED TO:							
	CHURCH TRANSFERRED FROM:							CHURCH TRANSFERRED TO:							
	CHURCH TRANSFERRED FROM:							CHURCH TRANSFERRED TO:							
	CHURCH TRANSFERRED FROM:							CHURCH TRANSFERRED TO:							

A-Asian   AA/B-African American/Black   H-Hispanic   N-Native American   P-Pacific Islander   W-White   MR-Multi-Racial   F-Female   M-Male

T-Transfer   OD-Other Denomination   PF-Profession of Christian Faith   R-Restored   CC-Charge Conf. Action   WD-Withdrawal   WC-Withdrawal under Charges   D-Death

PERMANENT CHURCH REGISTER

CHRONO-LOGICAL NUMBER	NAME			DATE OF BIRTH	RACIAL/ ETHNIC GROUP	GENDER	RECEIVED AS BAPTIZED MEMBER (B)		RECEIVED AS PROFESSING MEMBER (P)		REMOVED		B	P
	FAMILY	FIRST	MIDDLE				DATE	HOW	DATE	HOW	DATE	HOW		
	CHURCH TRANSFERRED FROM:						CHURCH TRANSFERRED TO:							
	CHURCH TRANSFERRED FROM:						CHURCH TRANSFERRED TO:							
	CHURCH TRANSFERRED FROM:						CHURCH TRANSFERRED TO:							
	CHURCH TRANSFERRED FROM:						CHURCH TRANSFERRED TO:							
	CHURCH TRANSFERRED FROM:						CHURCH TRANSFERRED TO:							
	CHURCH TRANSFERRED FROM:						CHURCH TRANSFERRED TO:							
	CHURCH TRANSFERRED FROM:						CHURCH TRANSFERRED TO:							
	CHURCH TRANSFERRED FROM:						CHURCH TRANSFERRED TO:							
	CHURCH TRANSFERRED FROM:						CHURCH TRANSFERRED TO:							

A-Asian AA/B-African American/Black H-Hispanic N-Native American P-Pacific Islander W-White MR-Multi-Racial F-Female M-Male

T-Transfer OD-Other Denomination PF-Profession of Christian Faith R-Restored CC-Charge Conf. Action WD-Withdrawal WC-Withdrawal under Charges D-Death

32

PERMANENT CHURCH REGISTER

CHRONO-LOGICAL NUMBER	NAME		DATE OF BIRTH	RACIAL/ETHNIC GROUP	GENDER	RECEIVED AS BAPTIZED MEMBER (B)			RECEIVED AS PROFESSING MEMBER (P)		REMOVED		B	P
	FAMILY	FIRST MIDDLE				DATE	HOW		DATE	HOW	DATE	HOW		
	CHURCH TRANSFERRED FROM:					CHURCH TRANSFERRED TO:								
	CHURCH TRANSFERRED FROM:					CHURCH TRANSFERRED TO:								
	CHURCH TRANSFERRED FROM:					CHURCH TRANSFERRED TO:								
	CHURCH TRANSFERRED FROM:					CHURCH TRANSFERRED TO:								
	CHURCH TRANSFERRED FROM:					CHURCH TRANSFERRED TO:								
	CHURCH TRANSFERRED FROM:					CHURCH TRANSFERRED TO:								
	CHURCH TRANSFERRED FROM:					CHURCH TRANSFERRED TO:								
	CHURCH TRANSFERRED FROM:					CHURCH TRANSFERRED TO:								
	CHURCH TRANSFERRED FROM:					CHURCH TRANSFERRED TO:								

A-Asian   AA/B-African American/Black   H-Hispanic   N-Native American   P-Pacific Islander   W-White   MR-Multi-Racial   F-Female   M-Male
T-Transfer   OD-Other Denomination   PF-Profession of Christian Faith   R-Restored   CC-Charge Conf. Action   WD-Withdrawal   WC-Withdrawal under Charges   D-Death

33

PERMANENT CHURCH REGISTER

CHRONO-LOGICAL NUMBER	NAME			DATE OF BIRTH	RACIAL/ ETHNIC GROUP	GENDER	RECEIVED AS BAPTIZED MEMBER (B)		RECEIVED AS PROFESSING MEMBER (P)		REMOVED		B	P
	FAMILY	FIRST	MIDDLE				DATE	HOW	DATE	HOW	DATE	HOW		
	CHURCH TRANSFERRED FROM:													
							CHURCH TRANSFERRED TO:							
	CHURCH TRANSFERRED FROM:													
							CHURCH TRANSFERRED TO:							
	CHURCH TRANSFERRED FROM:													
							CHURCH TRANSFERRED TO:							
	CHURCH TRANSFERRED FROM:													
							CHURCH TRANSFERRED TO:							
	CHURCH TRANSFERRED FROM:													
							CHURCH TRANSFERRED TO:							
	CHURCH TRANSFERRED FROM:													
							CHURCH TRANSFERRED TO:							
	CHURCH TRANSFERRED FROM:													
							CHURCH TRANSFERRED TO:							
	CHURCH TRANSFERRED FROM:													
							CHURCH TRANSFERRED TO:							
	CHURCH TRANSFERRED FROM:													
							CHURCH TRANSFERRED TO:							

A-Asian AA/B-African American/Black H-Hispanic N-Native American P-Pacific Islander W-White MR-Multi-Racial F-Female M-Male
T-Transfer OD-Other Denomination PF-Profession of Christian Faith R-Restored CC-Charge Conf. Action WD-Withdrawal WC-Withdrawal under Charges D-Death

PERMANENT CHURCH REGISTER

CHRONO-LOGICAL NUMBER	NAME			DATE OF BIRTH	RACIAL/ ETHNIC GROUP	GENDER	RECEIVED AS BAPTIZED MEMBER (B)		RECEIVED AS PROFESSING MEMBER (P)		REMOVED		B	P
	FAMILY	FIRST	MIDDLE				DATE	HOW	DATE	HOW	DATE	HOW		
	CHURCH TRANSFERRED FROM:						CHURCH TRANSFERRED TO:							
	CHURCH TRANSFERRED FROM:						CHURCH TRANSFERRED TO:							
	CHURCH TRANSFERRED FROM:						CHURCH TRANSFERRED TO:							
	CHURCH TRANSFERRED FROM:						CHURCH TRANSFERRED TO:							
	CHURCH TRANSFERRED FROM:						CHURCH TRANSFERRED TO:							
	CHURCH TRANSFERRED FROM:						CHURCH TRANSFERRED TO:							
	CHURCH TRANSFERRED FROM:						CHURCH TRANSFERRED TO:							
	CHURCH TRANSFERRED FROM:						CHURCH TRANSFERRED TO:							
	CHURCH TRANSFERRED FROM:						CHURCH TRANSFERRED TO:							

A-Asian   AA/B-African American/Black   H-Hispanic   N-Native American   P-Pacific Islander   W-White   MR-Multi-Racial   F-Female   M-Male
T-Transfer   OD-Other Denomination   PF-Profession of Christian Faith   R-Restored   CC-Charge Conf. Action   WD-Withdrawal   WC-Withdrawal under Charges   D-Death

PERMANENT CHURCH REGISTER

CHRONO-LOGICAL NUMBER	NAME			DATE OF BIRTH	RACIAL/ ETHNIC GROUP	GENDER	RECEIVED AS BAPTIZED MEMBER (B)		RECEIVED AS PROFESSING MEMBER (P)		REMOVED		B	P
	FAMILY	FIRST	MIDDLE				DATE	HOW	DATE	HOW	DATE	HOW		
	CHURCH TRANSFERRED FROM:						CHURCH TRANSFERRED TO:							
	CHURCH TRANSFERRED FROM:						CHURCH TRANSFERRED TO:							
	CHURCH TRANSFERRED FROM:						CHURCH TRANSFERRED TO:							
	CHURCH TRANSFERRED FROM:						CHURCH TRANSFERRED TO:							
	CHURCH TRANSFERRED FROM:						CHURCH TRANSFERRED TO:							
	CHURCH TRANSFERRED FROM:						CHURCH TRANSFERRED TO:							
	CHURCH TRANSFERRED FROM:						CHURCH TRANSFERRED TO:							
	CHURCH TRANSFERRED FROM:						CHURCH TRANSFERRED TO:							
	CHURCH TRANSFERRED FROM:						CHURCH TRANSFERRED TO:							

A-Asian   AA/B-African American/Black   H-Hispanic   N-Native American   P-Pacific Islander   W-White   MR-Multi-Racial   F-Female   M-Male

T-Transfer   OD-Other Denomination   PF-Profession of Christian Faith   R-Restored   CC-Charge Conf. Action   WD-Withdrawal   WC-Withdrawal under Charges   D-Death

PERMANENT CHURCH REGISTER

| CHRONO-LOGICAL NUMBER | NAME | | DATE OF BIRTH | RACIAL/ETHNIC GROUP | GENDER | RECEIVED AS BAPTIZED MEMBER (B) | | RECEIVED AS PROFESSING MEMBER (P) | | | REMOVED | | B | P |
	FAMILY	FIRST MIDDLE				DATE	HOW	DATE	HOW		DATE	HOW		
	CHURCH TRANSFERRED FROM:					CHURCH TRANSFERRED TO:								
	CHURCH TRANSFERRED FROM:					CHURCH TRANSFERRED TO:								
	CHURCH TRANSFERRED FROM:					CHURCH TRANSFERRED TO:								
	CHURCH TRANSFERRED FROM:					CHURCH TRANSFERRED TO:								
	CHURCH TRANSFERRED FROM:					CHURCH TRANSFERRED TO:								
	CHURCH TRANSFERRED FROM:					CHURCH TRANSFERRED TO:								
	CHURCH TRANSFERRED FROM:					CHURCH TRANSFERRED TO:								
	CHURCH TRANSFERRED FROM:					CHURCH TRANSFERRED TO:								
	CHURCH TRANSFERRED FROM:					CHURCH TRANSFERRED TO:								

A-Asian   AA/B-African American/Black   H-Hispanic   N-Native American   P-Pacific Islander   W-White   MR-Multi-Racial   F-Female   M-Male

T-Transfer   OD-Other Denomination   PF-Profession of Christian Faith   R-Restored   CC-Charge Conf. Action   WD-Withdrawal   WC-Withdrawal under Charges   D-Death

37

PERMANENT CHURCH REGISTER

| CHRONO-LOGICAL NUMBER | NAME | | DATE OF BIRTH | RACIAL/ETHNIC GROUP | GENDER | RECEIVED AS BAPTIZED MEMBER (B) | | RECEIVED AS PROFESSING MEMBER (P) | | REMOVED | | B | P |
	FAMILY	FIRST	MIDDLE				DATE	HOW	DATE	HOW	DATE	HOW		
	CHURCH TRANSFERRED FROM:							CHURCH TRANSFERRED TO:						
	CHURCH TRANSFERRED FROM:							CHURCH TRANSFERRED TO:						
	CHURCH TRANSFERRED FROM:							CHURCH TRANSFERRED TO:						
	CHURCH TRANSFERRED FROM:							CHURCH TRANSFERRED TO:						
	CHURCH TRANSFERRED FROM:							CHURCH TRANSFERRED TO:						
	CHURCH TRANSFERRED FROM:							CHURCH TRANSFERRED TO:						
	CHURCH TRANSFERRED FROM:							CHURCH TRANSFERRED TO:						
	CHURCH TRANSFERRED FROM:							CHURCH TRANSFERRED TO:						
	CHURCH TRANSFERRED FROM:							CHURCH TRANSFERRED TO:						

A-Asian   AA/B-African American/Black   H-Hispanic   N-Native American   P-Pacific Islander   W-White   MR-Multi-Racial   F-Female   M-Male

T-Transfer   OD-Other Denomination   PF-Profession of Christian Faith   R-Restored   CC-Charge Conf. Action   WD-Withdrawal   WC-Withdrawal under Charges   D-Death

PERMANENT CHURCH REGISTER

CHRONO-LOGICAL NUMBER	NAME			DATE OF BIRTH	RACIAL/ETHNIC GROUP	GENDER	RECEIVED AS BAPTIZED MEMBER (B)		RECEIVED AS PROFESSING MEMBER (P)		REMOVED		B	P
	FAMILY	FIRST	MIDDLE				DATE	HOW	DATE	HOW	DATE	HOW		
	CHURCH TRANSFERRED FROM:						CHURCH TRANSFERRED TO:							
	CHURCH TRANSFERRED FROM:						CHURCH TRANSFERRED TO:							
	CHURCH TRANSFERRED FROM:						CHURCH TRANSFERRED TO:							
	CHURCH TRANSFERRED FROM:						CHURCH TRANSFERRED TO:							
	CHURCH TRANSFERRED FROM:						CHURCH TRANSFERRED TO:							
	CHURCH TRANSFERRED FROM:						CHURCH TRANSFERRED TO:							
	CHURCH TRANSFERRED FROM:						CHURCH TRANSFERRED TO:							
	CHURCH TRANSFERRED FROM:						CHURCH TRANSFERRED TO:							
	CHURCH TRANSFERRED FROM:						CHURCH TRANSFERRED TO:							

A-Asian   AA/B-African American/Black   H-Hispanic   N-Native American   P-Pacific Islander   W-White   MR-Multi-Racial   F-Female   M-Male
T-Transfer   OD-Other Denomination   PF-Profession of Christian Faith   R-Restored   CC-Charge Conf. Action   WD-Withdrawal   WC-Withdrawal under Charges   D-Death

PERMANENT CHURCH REGISTER

CHRONO-LOGICAL NUMBER	NAME			DATE OF BIRTH	RACIAL/ ETHNIC GROUP	GENDER	RECEIVED AS BAPTIZED MEMBER (B)		RECEIVED AS PROFESSING MEMBER (P)		REMOVED		B	P
	FAMILY	FIRST	MIDDLE				DATE	HOW	DATE	HOW	DATE	HOW		
	CHURCH TRANSFERRED FROM:						CHURCH TRANSFERRED TO:							
	CHURCH TRANSFERRED FROM:						CHURCH TRANSFERRED TO:							
	CHURCH TRANSFERRED FROM:						CHURCH TRANSFERRED TO:							
	CHURCH TRANSFERRED FROM:						CHURCH TRANSFERRED TO:							
	CHURCH TRANSFERRED FROM:						CHURCH TRANSFERRED TO:							
	CHURCH TRANSFERRED FROM:						CHURCH TRANSFERRED TO:							
	CHURCH TRANSFERRED FROM:						CHURCH TRANSFERRED TO:							
	CHURCH TRANSFERRED FROM:						CHURCH TRANSFERRED TO:							
	CHURCH TRANSFERRED FROM:						CHURCH TRANSFERRED TO:							

A-Asian   AA/B-African American/Black   H-Hispanic   N-Native American   P-Pacific Islander   W-White   MR-Multi-Racial   F-Female   M-Male

T-Transfer   OD-Other Denomination   PF-Profession of Christian Faith   R-Restored   CC-Charge Conf. Action   WD-Withdrawal   WC-Withdrawal under Charges   D-Death

PERMANENT CHURCH REGISTER

CHRONO-LOGICAL NUMBER	NAME			DATE OF BIRTH	RACIAL/ ETHNIC GROUP	GENDER	RECEIVED AS BAPTIZED MEMBER (B)			RECEIVED AS PROFESSING MEMBER (P)			REMOVED		B	P
	FAMILY	FIRST	MIDDLE				DATE	HOW		DATE	HOW		DATE	HOW		
									CHURCH TRANSFERRED TO:							
	CHURCH TRANSFERRED FROM:															
									CHURCH TRANSFERRED TO:							
	CHURCH TRANSFERRED FROM:															
									CHURCH TRANSFERRED TO:							
	CHURCH TRANSFERRED FROM:															
									CHURCH TRANSFERRED TO:							
	CHURCH TRANSFERRED FROM:															
									CHURCH TRANSFERRED TO:							
	CHURCH TRANSFERRED FROM:															
									CHURCH TRANSFERRED TO:							
	CHURCH TRANSFERRED FROM:															
									CHURCH TRANSFERRED TO:							
	CHURCH TRANSFERRED FROM:															
									CHURCH TRANSFERRED TO:							
	CHURCH TRANSFERRED FROM:															
									CHURCH TRANSFERRED TO:							
	CHURCH TRANSFERRED FROM:															

A-Asian   AA/B-African American/Black   H-Hispanic   N-Native American   P-Pacific Islander   W-White   MR-Multi-Racial   F-Female   M-Male
T-Transfer   OD-Other Denomination   PF-Profession of Christian Faith   R-Restored   CC-Charge Conf. Action   WD-Withdrawal   WC-Withdrawal under Charges   D-Death

PERMANENT CHURCH REGISTER

| CHRONO-LOGICAL NUMBER | NAME | | | DATE OF BIRTH | RACIAL/ ETHNIC GROUP | GENDER | RECEIVED AS BAPTIZED MEMBER (B) | | | RECEIVED AS PROFESSING MEMBER (P) | | | REMOVED | | | B | P |
| | FAMILY | FIRST | MIDDLE | | | | DATE | HOW | | DATE | HOW | | DATE | HOW | | | |

CHURCH TRANSFERRED FROM: / CHURCH TRANSFERRED TO:

CHURCH TRANSFERRED FROM: / CHURCH TRANSFERRED TO:

CHURCH TRANSFERRED FROM: / CHURCH TRANSFERRED TO:

CHURCH TRANSFERRED FROM: / CHURCH TRANSFERRED TO:

CHURCH TRANSFERRED FROM: / CHURCH TRANSFERRED TO:

CHURCH TRANSFERRED FROM: / CHURCH TRANSFERRED TO:

CHURCH TRANSFERRED FROM: / CHURCH TRANSFERRED TO:

CHURCH TRANSFERRED FROM: / CHURCH TRANSFERRED TO:

CHURCH TRANSFERRED FROM: / CHURCH TRANSFERRED TO:

A-Asian   AA/B-African American/Black   H-Hispanic   N-Native American   P-Pacific Islander   W-White   MR-Multi-Racial   F-Female   M-Male
T-Transfer   OD-Other Denomination   PF-Profession of Christian Faith   R-Restored   CC-Charge Conf. Action   WD-Withdrawal   WC-Withdrawal under Charges   D-Death

42

PERMANENT CHURCH REGISTER

CHRONO-LOGICAL NUMBER	NAME			DATE OF BIRTH	RACIAL/ ETHNIC GROUP	GENDER	RECEIVED AS BAPTIZED MEMBER (B)			RECEIVED AS PROFESSING MEMBER (P)		REMOVED		B	P
	FAMILY	FIRST	MIDDLE				DATE	HOW		DATE	HOW	DATE	HOW		
	CHURCH TRANSFERRED FROM:						CHURCH TRANSFERRED TO:								
	CHURCH TRANSFERRED FROM:						CHURCH TRANSFERRED TO:								
	CHURCH TRANSFERRED FROM:						CHURCH TRANSFERRED TO:								
	CHURCH TRANSFERRED FROM:						CHURCH TRANSFERRED TO:								
	CHURCH TRANSFERRED FROM:						CHURCH TRANSFERRED TO:								
	CHURCH TRANSFERRED FROM:						CHURCH TRANSFERRED TO:								
	CHURCH TRANSFERRED FROM:						CHURCH TRANSFERRED TO:								
	CHURCH TRANSFERRED FROM:						CHURCH TRANSFERRED TO:								
	CHURCH TRANSFERRED FROM:						CHURCH TRANSFERRED TO:								

A-Asian AA/B-African American/Black H-Hispanic N-Native American P-Pacific Islander W-White MR-Multi-Racial F-Female M-Male
T-Transfer OD-Other Denomination PF-Profession of Christian Faith R-Restored CC-Charge Conf. Action WD-Withdrawal WC-Withdrawal under Charges D-Death

43

PERMANENT CHURCH REGISTER

CHRONO-LOGICAL NUMBER	NAME FAMILY	NAME FIRST	NAME MIDDLE	DATE OF BIRTH	RACIAL/ ETHNIC GROUP	GENDER	RECEIVED AS BAPTIZED MEMBER (B) DATE	RECEIVED AS BAPTIZED MEMBER (B) HOW	RECEIVED AS PROFESSING MEMBER (P) DATE	RECEIVED AS PROFESSING MEMBER (P) HOW	REMOVED DATE	REMOVED HOW	B	P
							CHURCH TRANSFERRED TO:							
	CHURCH TRANSFERRED FROM:													
							CHURCH TRANSFERRED TO:							
	CHURCH TRANSFERRED FROM:													
							CHURCH TRANSFERRED TO:							
	CHURCH TRANSFERRED FROM:													
							CHURCH TRANSFERRED TO:							
	CHURCH TRANSFERRED FROM:													
							CHURCH TRANSFERRED TO:							
	CHURCH TRANSFERRED FROM:													
							CHURCH TRANSFERRED TO:							
	CHURCH TRANSFERRED FROM:													
							CHURCH TRANSFERRED TO:							
	CHURCH TRANSFERRED FROM:													
							CHURCH TRANSFERRED TO:							
	CHURCH TRANSFERRED FROM:													
							CHURCH TRANSFERRED TO:							
	CHURCH TRANSFERRED FROM:													

A-Asian   AA/B-African American/Black   H-Hispanic   N-Native American   P-Pacific Islander   W-White   MR-Multi-Racial   F-Female   M-Male

T-Transfer   OD-Other Denomination   PF-Profession of Christian Faith   R-Restored   CC-Charge Conf. Action   WD-Withdrawal   WC-Withdrawal under Charges   D-Death

44

PERMANENT CHURCH REGISTER

| CHRONO-LOGICAL NUMBER | NAME | | DATE OF BIRTH | RACIAL/ETHNIC GROUP | GENDER | RECEIVED AS BAPTIZED MEMBER (B) | | RECEIVED AS PROFESSING MEMBER (P) | | | REMOVED | | B | P |
| | FAMILY | FIRST | MIDDLE | | | | DATE | HOW | DATE | HOW | | DATE | HOW | | |

	CHURCH TRANSFERRED FROM:								CHURCH TRANSFERRED TO:						
	CHURCH TRANSFERRED FROM:								CHURCH TRANSFERRED TO:						
	CHURCH TRANSFERRED FROM:								CHURCH TRANSFERRED TO:						
	CHURCH TRANSFERRED FROM:								CHURCH TRANSFERRED TO:						
	CHURCH TRANSFERRED FROM:								CHURCH TRANSFERRED TO:						
	CHURCH TRANSFERRED FROM:								CHURCH TRANSFERRED TO:						
	CHURCH TRANSFERRED FROM:								CHURCH TRANSFERRED TO:						
	CHURCH TRANSFERRED FROM:								CHURCH TRANSFERRED TO:						
	CHURCH TRANSFERRED FROM:								CHURCH TRANSFERRED TO:						

A-Asian   AA/B-African American/Black   H-Hispanic   N-Native American   P-Pacific Islander   W-White   MR-Multi-Racial   M-Male   F-Female
T-Transfer   OD-Other Denomination   PF-Profession of Christian Faith   R-Restored   CC-Charge Conf. Action   WD-Withdrawal   WC-Withdrawal under Charges   D-Death

45

PERMANENT CHURCH REGISTER

CHRONO-LOGICAL NUMBER	NAME			DATE OF BIRTH	RACIAL/ ETHNIC GROUP	GENDER	RECEIVED AS BAPTIZED MEMBER (B)		RECEIVED AS PROFESSING MEMBER (P)		REMOVED			
	FAMILY	FIRST	MIDDLE				DATE	HOW	DATE	HOW	DATE	HOW	B	P
	CHURCH TRANSFERRED FROM:						CHURCH TRANSFERRED TO:							
	CHURCH TRANSFERRED FROM:						CHURCH TRANSFERRED TO:							
	CHURCH TRANSFERRED FROM:						CHURCH TRANSFERRED TO:							
	CHURCH TRANSFERRED FROM:						CHURCH TRANSFERRED TO:							
	CHURCH TRANSFERRED FROM:						CHURCH TRANSFERRED TO:							
	CHURCH TRANSFERRED FROM:						CHURCH TRANSFERRED TO:							
	CHURCH TRANSFERRED FROM:						CHURCH TRANSFERRED TO:							
	CHURCH TRANSFERRED FROM:						CHURCH TRANSFERRED TO:							
	CHURCH TRANSFERRED FROM:						CHURCH TRANSFERRED TO:							

A-Asian   AA/B-African American/Black   H-Hispanic   N-Native American   P-Pacific Islander   W-White   MR-Multi-Racial   F-Female   M-Male

T-Transfer   OD-Other Denomination   PF-Profession of Christian Faith   R-Restored   CC-Charge Conf. Action   WD-Withdrawal   WC-Withdrawal under Charges   D-Death

PERMANENT CHURCH REGISTER

CHRONO-LOGICAL NUMBER	NAME			DATE OF BIRTH	RACIAL/ ETHNIC GROUP	GENDER	RECEIVED AS BAPTIZED MEMBER (B)		RECEIVED AS PROFESSING MEMBER (P)		REMOVED			
	FAMILY	FIRST	MIDDLE				DATE	HOW	DATE	HOW	DATE	HOW	B	P
	CHURCH TRANSFERRED FROM:						CHURCH TRANSFERRED TO:							
	CHURCH TRANSFERRED FROM:						CHURCH TRANSFERRED TO:							
	CHURCH TRANSFERRED FROM:						CHURCH TRANSFERRED TO:							
	CHURCH TRANSFERRED FROM:						CHURCH TRANSFERRED TO:							
	CHURCH TRANSFERRED FROM:						CHURCH TRANSFERRED TO:							
	CHURCH TRANSFERRED FROM:						CHURCH TRANSFERRED TO:							
	CHURCH TRANSFERRED FROM:						CHURCH TRANSFERRED TO:							
	CHURCH TRANSFERRED FROM:						CHURCH TRANSFERRED TO:							
	CHURCH TRANSFERRED FROM:						CHURCH TRANSFERRED TO:							

A-Asian AA/B-African American/Black H-Hispanic N-Native American P-Pacific Islander W-White MR-Multi-Racial M-Male F-Female

T-Transfer OD-Other Denomination PF-Profession of Christian Faith R-Restored CC-Charge Conf. Action WD-Withdrawal WC-Withdrawal under Charges D-Death

PERMANENT CHURCH REGISTER

CHRONO-LOGICAL NUMBER	NAME			DATE OF BIRTH	RACIAL/ ETHNIC GROUP	GENDER	RECEIVED AS BAPTIZED MEMBER (B)			RECEIVED AS PROFESSING MEMBER (P)			REMOVED		B	P
	FAMILY	FIRST	MIDDLE				DATE	HOW		DATE	HOW		DATE	HOW		
	CHURCH TRANSFERRED FROM:						CHURCH TRANSFERRED TO:									
	CHURCH TRANSFERRED FROM:						CHURCH TRANSFERRED TO:									
	CHURCH TRANSFERRED FROM:						CHURCH TRANSFERRED TO:									
	CHURCH TRANSFERRED FROM:						CHURCH TRANSFERRED TO:									
	CHURCH TRANSFERRED FROM:						CHURCH TRANSFERRED TO:									
	CHURCH TRANSFERRED FROM:						CHURCH TRANSFERRED TO:									
	CHURCH TRANSFERRED FROM:						CHURCH TRANSFERRED TO:									
	CHURCH TRANSFERRED FROM:						CHURCH TRANSFERRED TO:									
	CHURCH TRANSFERRED FROM:						CHURCH TRANSFERRED TO:									

A-Asian   AA/B-African American/Black   H-Hispanic   N-Native American   P-Pacific Islander   W-White   MR-Multi-Racial   F-Female   M-Male

T-Transfer   OD-Other Denomination   PF-Profession of Christian Faith   R-Restored   CC-Charge Conf. Action   WD-Withdrawal   WC-Withdrawal under Charges   D-Death

48

PERMANENT CHURCH REGISTER

CHRONO-LOGICAL NUMBER	NAME			DATE OF BIRTH	RACIAL/ ETHNIC GROUP	GENDER	RECEIVED AS BAPTIZED MEMBER (B)			RECEIVED AS PROFESSING MEMBER (P)			REMOVED		B	P
	FAMILY	FIRST	MIDDLE				DATE	HOW		DATE	HOW		DATE	HOW		
									CHURCH TRANSFERRED TO:							
	CHURCH TRANSFERRED FROM:															
									CHURCH TRANSFERRED TO:							
	CHURCH TRANSFERRED FROM:															
									CHURCH TRANSFERRED TO:							
	CHURCH TRANSFERRED FROM:															
									CHURCH TRANSFERRED TO:							
	CHURCH TRANSFERRED FROM:															
									CHURCH TRANSFERRED TO:							
	CHURCH TRANSFERRED FROM:															
									CHURCH TRANSFERRED TO:							
	CHURCH TRANSFERRED FROM:															
									CHURCH TRANSFERRED TO:							
	CHURCH TRANSFERRED FROM:															
									CHURCH TRANSFERRED TO:							
	CHURCH TRANSFERRED FROM:															
									CHURCH TRANSFERRED TO:							
	CHURCH TRANSFERRED FROM:															

A-Asian   AA/B-African American/Black   H-Hispanic   N-Native American   P-Pacific Islander   W-White   MR-Multi-Racial   F-Female   M-Male

T-Transfer   OD-Other Denomination   PF-Profession of Christian Faith   R-Restored   CC-Charge Conf. Action   WD-Withdrawal   WC-Withdrawal under Charges   D-Death

49

PERMANENT CHURCH REGISTER

CHRONO-LOGICAL NUMBER	NAME — FAMILY / FIRST / MIDDLE	DATE OF BIRTH	RACIAL/ETHNIC GROUP	GENDER	RECEIVED AS BAPTIZED MEMBER (B) — DATE	HOW	RECEIVED AS PROFESSING MEMBER (P) — DATE	HOW	REMOVED — DATE	HOW	B	P
	CHURCH TRANSFERRED FROM:				CHURCH TRANSFERRED TO:							
	CHURCH TRANSFERRED FROM:				CHURCH TRANSFERRED TO:							
	CHURCH TRANSFERRED FROM:				CHURCH TRANSFERRED TO:							
	CHURCH TRANSFERRED FROM:				CHURCH TRANSFERRED TO:							
	CHURCH TRANSFERRED FROM:				CHURCH TRANSFERRED TO:							
	CHURCH TRANSFERRED FROM:				CHURCH TRANSFERRED TO:							
	CHURCH TRANSFERRED FROM:				CHURCH TRANSFERRED TO:							
	CHURCH TRANSFERRED FROM:				CHURCH TRANSFERRED TO:							
	CHURCH TRANSFERRED FROM:				CHURCH TRANSFERRED TO:							

A-Asian   AA/B-African American/Black   H-Hispanic   N-Native American   P-Pacific Islander   W-White   MR-Multi-Racial   M-Male   F-Female

T-Transfer   OD-Other Denomination   PF-Profession of Christian Faith   R-Restored   CC-Charge Conf. Action   WD-Withdrawal   WC-Withdrawal under Charges   D-Death

PERMANENT CHURCH REGISTER

CHRONO-LOGICAL NUMBER	NAME			DATE OF BIRTH	RACIAL/ ETHNIC GROUP	GENDER	RECEIVED AS BAPTIZED MEMBER (B)			RECEIVED AS PROFESSING MEMBER (P)			REMOVED		B	P
	FAMILY	FIRST	MIDDLE				DATE	HOW		DATE	HOW		DATE	HOW		

CHURCH TRANSFERRED FROM: / CHURCH TRANSFERRED TO:
(repeated for each member row)

A-Asian   AA/B-African American/Black   H-Hispanic   N-Native American   P-Pacific Islander   W-White   MR-Multi-Racial   F-Female   M-Male
T-Transfer   OD-Other Denomination   PF-Profession of Christian Faith   R-Restored   CC-Charge Conf. Action   WD-Withdrawal   WC-Withdrawal under Charges   D-Death

PERMANENT CHURCH REGISTER

CHRONO-LOGICAL NUMBER	NAME			DATE OF BIRTH	RACIAL/ETHNIC GROUP	GENDER	RECEIVED AS BAPTIZED MEMBER (B)		RECEIVED AS PROFESSING MEMBER (P)		REMOVED		B	P
	FAMILY	FIRST	MIDDLE				DATE	HOW	DATE	HOW	DATE	HOW		
		CHURCH TRANSFERRED FROM:					CHURCH TRANSFERRED TO:							
		CHURCH TRANSFERRED FROM:					CHURCH TRANSFERRED TO:							
		CHURCH TRANSFERRED FROM:					CHURCH TRANSFERRED TO:							
		CHURCH TRANSFERRED FROM:					CHURCH TRANSFERRED TO:							
		CHURCH TRANSFERRED FROM:					CHURCH TRANSFERRED TO:							
		CHURCH TRANSFERRED FROM:					CHURCH TRANSFERRED TO:							
		CHURCH TRANSFERRED FROM:					CHURCH TRANSFERRED TO:							
		CHURCH TRANSFERRED FROM:					CHURCH TRANSFERRED TO:							
		CHURCH TRANSFERRED FROM:					CHURCH TRANSFERRED TO:							

A-Asian   AA/B-African American/Black   H-Hispanic   N-Native American   P-Pacific Islander   W-White   MR-Multi-Racial   F-Female   M-Male

T-Transfer   OD-Other Denomination   PF-Profession of Christian Faith   R-Restored   CC-Charge Conf. Action   WD-Withdrawal   WC-Withdrawal under Charges   D-Death

52

PERMANENT CHURCH REGISTER

CHRONO-LOGICAL NUMBER	NAME		DATE OF BIRTH	RACIAL/ ETHNIC GROUP	GENDER	RECEIVED AS BAPTIZED MEMBER (B)		RECEIVED AS PROFESSING MEMBER (P)		REMOVED		B	P
	FIRST	MIDDLE				DATE	HOW	DATE	HOW	DATE	HOW		
	FAMILY					CHURCH TRANSFERRED FROM:		CHURCH TRANSFERRED TO:					
						CHURCH TRANSFERRED FROM:		CHURCH TRANSFERRED TO:					
						CHURCH TRANSFERRED FROM:		CHURCH TRANSFERRED TO:					
						CHURCH TRANSFERRED FROM:		CHURCH TRANSFERRED TO:					
						CHURCH TRANSFERRED FROM:		CHURCH TRANSFERRED TO:					
						CHURCH TRANSFERRED FROM:		CHURCH TRANSFERRED TO:					
						CHURCH TRANSFERRED FROM:		CHURCH TRANSFERRED TO:					
						CHURCH TRANSFERRED FROM:		CHURCH TRANSFERRED TO:					
						CHURCH TRANSFERRED FROM:		CHURCH TRANSFERRED TO:					

A-Asian   AA/B-African American/Black   H-Hispanic   N-Native American   P-Pacific Islander   W-White   MR-Multi-Racial   F-Female   M-Male

T-Transfer   OD-Other Denomination   PF-Profession of Christian Faith   R-Restored   CC-Charge Conf. Action   WD-Withdrawal   WC-Withdrawal under Charges   D-Death

PERMANENT CHURCH REGISTER

CHRONOLOGICAL NUMBER	NAME FAMILY	FIRST	MIDDLE	DATE OF BIRTH	RACIAL/ETHNIC GROUP	GENDER	RECEIVED AS BAPTIZED MEMBER (B) DATE	HOW	RECEIVED AS PROFESSING MEMBER (P) DATE	HOW	REMOVED DATE	HOW	B	P
	CHURCH TRANSFERRED FROM:						CHURCH TRANSFERRED TO:							
	CHURCH TRANSFERRED FROM:						CHURCH TRANSFERRED TO:							
	CHURCH TRANSFERRED FROM:						CHURCH TRANSFERRED TO:							
	CHURCH TRANSFERRED FROM:						CHURCH TRANSFERRED TO:							
	CHURCH TRANSFERRED FROM:						CHURCH TRANSFERRED TO:							
	CHURCH TRANSFERRED FROM:						CHURCH TRANSFERRED TO:							
	CHURCH TRANSFERRED FROM:						CHURCH TRANSFERRED TO:							
	CHURCH TRANSFERRED FROM:						CHURCH TRANSFERRED TO:							
	CHURCH TRANSFERRED FROM:						CHURCH TRANSFERRED TO:							

A-Asian   AA/B-African American/Black   H-Hispanic   N-Native American   P-Pacific Islander   W-White   MR-Multi-Racial   F-Female   M-Male
T-Transfer   OD-Other Denomination   PF-Profession of Christian Faith   R-Restored   CC-Charge Conf. Action   WD-Withdrawal   WC-Withdrawal under Charges   D-Death

54

PERMANENT CHURCH REGISTER

CHRONO-LOGICAL NUMBER	NAME			DATE OF BIRTH	RACIAL/ ETHNIC GROUP	GENDER	RECEIVED AS BAPTIZED MEMBER (B)			RECEIVED AS PROFESSING MEMBER (P)			REMOVED		B	P
	FAMILY	FIRST	MIDDLE				DATE	HOW		DATE	HOW		DATE	HOW		
	CHURCH TRANSFERRED FROM:						CHURCH TRANSFERRED TO:									
	CHURCH TRANSFERRED FROM:						CHURCH TRANSFERRED TO:									
	CHURCH TRANSFERRED FROM:						CHURCH TRANSFERRED TO:									
	CHURCH TRANSFERRED FROM:						CHURCH TRANSFERRED TO:									
	CHURCH TRANSFERRED FROM:						CHURCH TRANSFERRED TO:									
	CHURCH TRANSFERRED FROM:						CHURCH TRANSFERRED TO:									
	CHURCH TRANSFERRED FROM:						CHURCH TRANSFERRED TO:									
	CHURCH TRANSFERRED FROM:						CHURCH TRANSFERRED TO:									
	CHURCH TRANSFERRED FROM:						CHURCH TRANSFERRED TO:									

A-Asian   AA/B-African American/Black   H-Hispanic   N-Native American   P-Pacific Islander   W-White   MR-Multi-Racial   F-Female   M-Male
T-Transfer   OD-Other Denomination   PF-Profession of Christian Faith   R-Restored   CC-Charge Conf. Action   WD-Withdrawal   WC-Withdrawal under Charges   D-Death

PERMANENT CHURCH REGISTER

CHRONO-LOGICAL NUMBER	NAME			DATE OF BIRTH	RACIAL/ETHNIC GROUP	GENDER	RECEIVED AS BAPTIZED MEMBER (B)		RECEIVED AS PROFESSING MEMBER (P)			REMOVED		B	P
	FAMILY	FIRST	MIDDLE				DATE	HOW	DATE	HOW		DATE	HOW		

CHURCH TRANSFERRED FROM: CHURCH TRANSFERRED TO:

CHURCH TRANSFERRED FROM: CHURCH TRANSFERRED TO:

CHURCH TRANSFERRED FROM: CHURCH TRANSFERRED TO:

CHURCH TRANSFERRED FROM: CHURCH TRANSFERRED TO:

CHURCH TRANSFERRED FROM: CHURCH TRANSFERRED TO:

CHURCH TRANSFERRED FROM: CHURCH TRANSFERRED TO:

CHURCH TRANSFERRED FROM: CHURCH TRANSFERRED TO:

CHURCH TRANSFERRED FROM: CHURCH TRANSFERRED TO:

CHURCH TRANSFERRED FROM: CHURCH TRANSFERRED TO:

A-Asian   AA/B-African American/Black   H-Hispanic   N-Native American   P-Pacific Islander   W-White   MR-Multi-Racial   F-Female   M-Male

T-Transfer   OD-Other Denomination   PF-Profession of Christian Faith   R-Restored   CC-Charge Conf. Action   PF-Profession of Christian Faith   WD-Withdrawal   WC-Withdrawal under Charges   D-Death

PERMANENT CHURCH REGISTER

| CHRONO-LOGICAL NUMBER | NAME | | | DATE OF BIRTH | RACIAL/ ETHNIC GROUP | GENDER | RECEIVED AS BAPTIZED MEMBER (B) | | RECEIVED AS PROFESSING MEMBER (P) | | REMOVED | | B | P |
	FAMILY	FIRST	MIDDLE				DATE	HOW	DATE	HOW	DATE	HOW		
	CHURCH TRANSFERRED FROM:						CHURCH TRANSFERRED TO:							
	CHURCH TRANSFERRED FROM:						CHURCH TRANSFERRED TO:							
	CHURCH TRANSFERRED FROM:						CHURCH TRANSFERRED TO:							
	CHURCH TRANSFERRED FROM:						CHURCH TRANSFERRED TO:							
	CHURCH TRANSFERRED FROM:						CHURCH TRANSFERRED TO:							
	CHURCH TRANSFERRED FROM:						CHURCH TRANSFERRED TO:							
	CHURCH TRANSFERRED FROM:						CHURCH TRANSFERRED TO:							
	CHURCH TRANSFERRED FROM:						CHURCH TRANSFERRED TO:							
	CHURCH TRANSFERRED FROM:						CHURCH TRANSFERRED TO:							

A-Asian   AA/B-African American/Black   H-Hispanic   N-Native American   P-Pacific Islander   W-White   MR-Multi-Racial   F-Female   M-Male

T-Transfer   OD-Other Denomination   PF-Profession of Christian Faith   R-Restored   CC-Charge Conf. Action   WD-Withdrawal   WC-Withdrawal under Charges   D-Death

PERMANENT CHURCH REGISTER

CHRONO-LOGICAL NUMBER	NAME		DATE OF BIRTH	RACIAL/ETHNIC GROUP	GENDER	RECEIVED AS BAPTIZED MEMBER (B)			RECEIVED AS PROFESSING MEMBER (P)			REMOVED		B	P
	FAMILY	FIRST / MIDDLE				DATE	HOW		DATE	HOW		DATE	HOW		
	CHURCH TRANSFERRED FROM:					CHURCH TRANSFERRED TO:									
	CHURCH TRANSFERRED FROM:					CHURCH TRANSFERRED TO:									
	CHURCH TRANSFERRED FROM:					CHURCH TRANSFERRED TO:									
	CHURCH TRANSFERRED FROM:					CHURCH TRANSFERRED TO:									
	CHURCH TRANSFERRED FROM:					CHURCH TRANSFERRED TO:									
	CHURCH TRANSFERRED FROM:					CHURCH TRANSFERRED TO:									
	CHURCH TRANSFERRED FROM:					CHURCH TRANSFERRED TO:									
	CHURCH TRANSFERRED FROM:					CHURCH TRANSFERRED TO:									
	CHURCH TRANSFERRED FROM:					CHURCH TRANSFERRED TO:									

A-Asian   AA/B-African American/Black   H-Hispanic   N-Native American   P-Pacific Islander   W-White   MR-Multi-Racial   F-Female   M-Male

T-Transfer   OD-Other Denomination   PF-Profession of Christian Faith   CC-Charge Conf. Action   R-Restored   WD-Withdrawal   WC-Withdrawal under Charges   D-Death

PERMANENT CHURCH REGISTER

| CHRONO-LOGICAL NUMBER | NAME | | DATE OF BIRTH | RACIAL/ETHNIC GROUP | GENDER | RECEIVED AS BAPTIZED MEMBER (B) | | RECEIVED AS PROFESSING MEMBER (P) | | REMOVED | | B | P |
	FAMILY	FIRST / MIDDLE				DATE	HOW	DATE	HOW	DATE	HOW		
	CHURCH TRANSFERRED FROM:					CHURCH TRANSFERRED TO:							
	CHURCH TRANSFERRED FROM:					CHURCH TRANSFERRED TO:							
	CHURCH TRANSFERRED FROM:					CHURCH TRANSFERRED TO:							
	CHURCH TRANSFERRED FROM:					CHURCH TRANSFERRED TO:							
	CHURCH TRANSFERRED FROM:					CHURCH TRANSFERRED TO:							
	CHURCH TRANSFERRED FROM:					CHURCH TRANSFERRED TO:							
	CHURCH TRANSFERRED FROM:					CHURCH TRANSFERRED TO:							
	CHURCH TRANSFERRED FROM:					CHURCH TRANSFERRED TO:							
	CHURCH TRANSFERRED FROM:					CHURCH TRANSFERRED TO:							

A-Asian   AA/B-African American/Black   H-Hispanic   N-Native American   P-Pacific Islander   W-White   MR-Multi-Racial   M-Male   F-Female

T-Transfer   OD-Other Denomination   PF-Profession of Christian Faith   R-Restored   CC-Charge Conf. Action   WD-Withdrawal   WC-Withdrawal under Charges   D-Death

CONSTITUENCY ROLL
(Required)

A constituency roll includes the names and addresses of persons who are not members of the church, including unbaptized children, church school members, and other nonmembers for whom the local church has pastoral responsibility (¶230.3).

This record is required by *The Book of Discipline* for each church (¶230). The responsibility rests with the pastor to report its status to the annual conference (¶ 232).

The membership secretary is directed to provide this and other lists to the Church Council regularly (¶234).

The current list of addresses provides a working list for church growth and ministry. The flexibility added by the ability to remove these pages helps with record keeping.

The "Removed" column includes both how and the date. Removal may be by B (Baptized Membership), P (Professing Membership), D (Death) or W (Withdrawal).

Prepared and edited by the General Council on Finance and Administration. Published by The United Methodist Publishing House, Nashville, Tennessee.

CONSTITUENCY ROLL

NAME	ADDRESS	DATE OF BIRTH	REMOVED	
			DATE	HOW

P-Professing Member   B-Baptized Member   D-Death   W-Withdrawal

61

CONSTITUENCY ROLL

NAME	ADDRESS	DATE OF BIRTH	REMOVED	
			DATE	HOW

P-Professing Member   B-Baptized Member   D-Death   W-Withdrawal

CONSTITUENCY ROLL

NAME	ADDRESS	DATE OF BIRTH	REMOVED	
			DATE	HOW

P-Professing Member   B-Baptized Member   D-Death   W-Withdrawal

CONSTITUENCY ROLL

NAME	ADDRESS	DATE OF BIRTH	REMOVED	
			DATE	HOW

P-Professing Member   B-Baptized Member   D-Death   W-Withdrawal

CONSTITUENCY ROLL

NAME	ADDRESS	DATE OF BIRTH	REMOVED	
			DATE	HOW

P-Professing Member   B-Baptized Member   D-Death   W-Withdrawal

CONSTITUENCY ROLL

NAME	ADDRESS	DATE OF BIRTH	REMOVED	
			DATE	HOW

P-Professing Member   B-Baptized Member   D-Death   W-Withdrawal

CONSTITUENCY ROLL

NAME	ADDRESS	DATE OF BIRTH	REMOVED	
			DATE	HOW

P-Professing Member   B-Baptized Member   D-Death   W-Withdrawal

AFFILIATE/ASSOCIATE MEMBER ROLL
(Required)

The Affiliate/Associate Member Roll can assist the pastor, membership secretary, and Church Council Membership Audit Committee in auditing and caring for persons in these categories.

An *Affiliate member*, as described in *The Book of Discipline* (¶227) is a permanent full member of a "United Methodist Church, of an affiliated autonomous Methodist or united church, or of a Methodist church that has a concordat agreement with The United Methodist Church, who resides for an extended period in a city or community at a distance from the member's home church." Students, military service personnel, and retired persons who maintain two residences fall in this category.

Associate members are temporary residents who want to maintain their memberships in a church of another denomination but desire to be active participants in a local United Methodist church.

Prepared and edited by the General Council on Finance and Administration. Published by The United Methodist Publishing House, Nashville, Tennessee.

AFFILIATE/ASSOCIATE MEMBER ROLL

NAME	LOCAL ADDRESS	OTHER ADDRESS	AFFILIATE/ASSOCIATE MEMBER			HOME CHURCH
			TYPE	Date Received	Date Removed	

AF-Affiliate Member   AS-Associate Member

69

PROFESSING MEMBERS REMOVED BY CHARGE CONFERENCE ACTION
(Required)

The Book of Discipline requires that a cumulative record be maintained of persons removed by action of the charge conference. It is the responsibility of the pastor, with the assistance of the membership secretary, to keep this record current and to advise the charge conference and the Church Council of its contents annually.

The chronological reference number provides a cross-reference to the information on the permanent church register.

The last known address may be easily outdated unless the process of annual review is followed. Some removed members may still reside in the local community. Sharing addresses with the witness ministries or evangelism ministry group may help attract members who are inactive or who are former members of the church.

The column "Reason for Removal" should indicate either CC (charge conference action), or W (withdrawal by request).

The Book of Discipline describes the procedure to reinstate and transfer persons from this roll (¶228.2b). The column on restoration and transfer should be completed with date and place.

Prepared and edited by the General Council on Finance and Administration. Published by The United Methodist Publishing House, Nashville, Tennessee.

PROFESSING MEMBERS REMOVED BY CHARGE CONFERENCE ACTION

Chronological Reference Number	Date of Final Charge Conference Action	NAME	LAST KNOWN ADDRESS	REASON FOR REMOVAL	RESTORED/ TRANSFERRED

CC-Charge Conference Action   W-Withdrawal

1

PROFESSING MEMBERS REMOVED BY CHARGE CONFERENCE ACTION

Chronological Reference Number	Date of Final Charge Conference Action	NAME	LAST KNOWN ADDRESS	REASON FOR REMOVAL	RESTORED/ TRANSFERRED

CC-Charge Conference Action   W-Withdrawal

72

PROFESSING MEMBERS REMOVED BY CHARGE CONFERENCE ACTION

Chronological Reference Number	Date of Final Charge Conference Action	NAME	LAST KNOWN ADDRESS	REASON FOR REMOVAL	RESTORED/ TRANSFERRED

CC-Charge Conference Action   W-Withdrawal

73

HISTORICAL RECORD
(Recommended)

This section provides space for pertinent data about the history of the church and congregation.
Suggestions include:
Dates of capital improvements
Major anniversaries and celebrations
Significant programs offered to the community
A list of organists, directors of Christian education, and others
Organization of senior citizens center
Organization of day-care center
Dates of mergers or relocation
Disasters—tornadoes, floods, fire, and other

Prepared and edited by the General Council on Finance and Administration. Published by The United Methodist Publishing House, Nashville, Tennessee.

HISTORICAL RECORD

HISTORICAL RECORD

HISTORICAL RECORD

RECORD OF MARRIAGES
(Recommended)

Every wedding performed by the pastor(s) of the church should be entered.

The column for church relationship clarifies how or if these persons are involved with the life of the local church.

The former address (prenuptial) will help identify households, while the new address will be important for pastoral care for church records.

The information on issuance of the license will provide a cross-reference for legal papers and also provide historical and permanent data.

Prepared and edited by the General Council on Finance and Administration. Published by The United Methodist Publishing House, Nashville, Tennessee.

RECORD OF MARRIAGES

FAMILY	FULL NAME FIRST	MID-	ADDRESS	CHURCH RELATION-SHIP	OFFICIANT, DATE, AND PLACE OF MARRIAGE			LICENSE ISSUED BY			NEW ADDRESS
Man					Pastor	Date	Place	County	State	License Number	
Woman											
Man					Pastor	Date	Place	County	State	License Number	
Woman											
Man					Pastor	Date	Place	County	State	License Number	
Woman											
Man					Pastor	Date	Place	County	State	License Number	
Woman											
Man					Pastor	Date	Place	County	State	License Number	
Woman											
Man					Pastor	Date	Place	County	State	License Number	
Woman											
Man					Pastor	Date	Place	County	State	License Number	
Woman											
Man					Pastor	Date	Place	County	State	License Number	
Woman											
Man					Pastor	Date	Place	County	State	License Number	
Woman											

B-Baptized Member   P-Professing Member   AF-Affiliate Member   AS-Associate Member   CR-Constituency Roll

RECORD OF MARRIAGES

FULL NAME		ADDRESS	CHURCH RELATION-SHIP	OFFICIANT, DATE, AND PLACE OF MARRIAGE	LICENSE ISSUED BY	NEW ADDRESS
FAMILY	FIRST	MID-				
Man				Pastor	County	
				Date	State	
Woman				Place	License Number	
Man				Pastor	County	
				Date	State	
Woman				Place	License Number	
Man				Pastor	County	
				Date	State	
Woman				Place	License Number	
Man				Pastor	County	
				Date	State	
Woman				Place	License Number	
Man				Pastor	County	
				Date	State	
Woman				Place	License Number	
Man				Pastor	County	
				Date	State	
Woman				Place	License Number	
Man				Pastor	County	
				Date	State	
Woman				Place	License Number	
Man				Pastor	County	
				Date	State	
Woman				Place	License Number	
Man				Pastor	County	
				Date	State	
Woman				Place	License Number	

B-Baptized Member P-Professing Member AF-Affiliate Member AS-Associate Member CR-Constituency Roll

RECORD OF MARRIAGES

FULL NAME			ADDRESS	CHURCH RELATION-SHIP	OFFICIANT, DATE, AND PLACE OF MARRIAGE	LICENSE ISSUED BY	NEW ADDRESS
FAMILY	FIRST	MID-					
Man					Pastor / Date / Place	County / State / License Number	
Woman							
Man					Pastor / Date / Place	County / State / License Number	
Woman							
Man					Pastor / Date / Place	County / State / License Number	
Woman							
Man					Pastor / Date / Place	County / State / License Number	
Woman							
Man					Pastor / Date / Place	County / State / License Number	
Woman							
Man					Pastor / Date / Place	County / State / License Number	
Woman							
Man					Pastor / Date / Place	County / State / License Number	
Woman							
Man					Pastor / Date / Place	County / State / License Number	
Woman							
Man					Pastor / Date / Place	County / State / License Number	
Woman							

B-Baptized Member   P-Professing Member   AF-Affiliate Member   AS-Associate Member   CR-Constituency Roll

RECORD OF MARRIAGES

FAMILY	FIRST	MID-	ADDRESS	CHURCH RELATION-SHIP	OFFICIANT, DATE, AND PLACE OF MARRIAGE			LICENSE ISSUED BY			NEW ADDRESS
Man					Pastor	Date	Place	County	State	License Number	
Woman											
Man					Pastor	Date	Place	County	State	License Number	
Woman											
Man					Pastor	Date	Place	County	State	License Number	
Woman											
Man					Pastor	Date	Place	County	State	License Number	
Woman											
Man					Pastor	Date	Place	County	State	License Number	
Woman											
Man					Pastor	Date	Place	County	State	License Number	
Woman											
Man					Pastor	Date	Place	County	State	License Number	
Woman											
Man					Pastor	Date	Place	County	State	License Number	
Woman											
Man					Pastor	Date	Place	County	State	License Number	
Woman											

B-Baptized Member   P-Professing Member   AF-Affiliate Member   AS-Associate Member   CR-Constituency Roll

RECORD OF MARRIAGES

FAMILY	FULL NAME FIRST	MID-	ADDRESS	CHURCH RELATION-SHIP	OFFICIANT, DATE, AND PLACE OF MARRIAGE	LICENSE ISSUED BY	NEW ADDRESS
Man					Pastor	County	
					Date	State	
Woman					Place	License Number	
Man					Pastor	County	
					Date	State	
Woman					Place	License Number	
Man					Pastor	County	
					Date	State	
Woman					Place	License Number	
Man					Pastor	County	
					Date	State	
Woman					Place	License Number	
Man					Pastor	County	
					Date	State	
Woman					Place	License Number	
Man					Pastor	County	
					Date	State	
Woman					Place	License Number	
Man					Pastor	County	
					Date	State	
Woman					Place	License Number	
Man					Pastor	County	
					Date	State	
Woman					Place	License Number	
Man					Pastor	County	
					Date	State	
Woman					Place	License Number	

B-Baptized Member   P-Professing Member   AF-Affiliate Member   AS-Associate Member   CR-Constituency Roll

RECORD OF MARRIAGES

FAMILY	FULL NAME FIRST	MID-	ADDRESS	CHURCH RELATION-SHIP	OFFICIANT, DATE, AND PLACE OF MARRIAGE	LICENSE ISSUED BY	NEW ADDRESS
Man					Pastor	County	
					Date	State	
Woman					Place	License Number	
Man					Pastor	County	
					Date	State	
Woman					Place	License Number	
Man					Pastor	County	
					Date	State	
Woman					Place	License Number	
Man					Pastor	County	
					Date	State	
Woman					Place	License Number	
Man					Pastor	County	
					Date	State	
Woman					Place	License Number	
Man					Pastor	County	
					Date	State	
Woman					Place	License Number	
Man					Pastor	County	
					Date	State	
Woman					Place	License Number	
Man					Pastor	County	
					Date	State	
Woman					Place	License Number	
Man					Pastor	County	
					Date	State	
Woman					Place	License Number	

B-Baptized Member   P-Professing Member   AF-Affiliate Member   AS-Associate Member   CR-Constituency Roll

84

RECORD OF MARRIAGES

FAMILY	FIRST	MID-	ADDRESS	CHURCH RELATION-SHIP	OFFICIANT, DATE, AND PLACE OF MARRIAGE	LICENSE ISSUED BY	NEW ADDRESS
Man					Pastor	County	
					Date	State	
					Place	License Number	
Woman							
Man					Pastor	County	
					Date	State	
					Place	License Number	
Woman							
Man					Pastor	County	
					Date	State	
					Place	License Number	
Woman							
Man					Pastor	County	
					Date	State	
					Place	License Number	
Woman							
Man					Pastor	County	
					Date	State	
					Place	License Number	
Woman							
Man					Pastor	County	
					Date	State	
					Place	License Number	
Woman							
Man					Pastor	County	
					Date	State	
					Place	License Number	
Woman							
Man					Pastor	County	
					Date	State	
					Place	License Number	
Woman							
Man					Pastor	County	
					Date	State	
					Place	License Number	
Woman							

B-Baptized Member   P-Professing Member   AF-Affiliate Member   AS-Associate Member   CR-Constituency Roll

RECORD OF MARRIAGES

FAMILY	FULL NAME		ADDRESS	CHURCH RELATION-SHIP	OFFICIANT, DATE, AND PLACE OF MARRIAGE	LICENSE ISSUED BY	NEW ADDRESS
	FIRST	MID-					
Man					Pastor	County	
					Date	State	
Woman					Place	License Number	
Man					Pastor	County	
					Date	State	
Woman					Place	License Number	
Man					Pastor	County	
					Date	State	
Woman					Place	License Number	
Man					Pastor	County	
					Date	State	
Woman					Place	License Number	
Man					Pastor	County	
					Date	State	
Woman					Place	License Number	
Man					Pastor	County	
					Date	State	
Woman					Place	License Number	
Man					Pastor	County	
					Date	State	
Woman					Place	License Number	
Man					Pastor	County	
					Date	State	
Woman					Place	License Number	

B-Baptized Member   P-Professing Member   AF-Affiliate Member   AS-Associate Member   CR-Constituency Roll

RECORD OF MARRIAGES

FAMILY	FULL NAME FIRST	MID-	ADDRESS	CHURCH RELATION-SHIP	OFFICIANT, DATE, AND PLACE OF MARRIAGE		LICENSE ISSUED BY		NEW ADDRESS
Man					Pastor		County		
					Date		State		
Woman					Place		License Number		
Man					Pastor		County		
					Date		State		
Woman					Place		License Number		
Man					Pastor		County		
					Date		State		
Woman					Place		License Number		
Man					Pastor		County		
					Date		State		
Woman					Place		License Number		
Man					Pastor		County		
					Date		State		
Woman					Place		License Number		
Man					Pastor		County		
					Date		State		
Woman					Place		License Number		
Man					Pastor		County		
					Date		State		
Woman					Place		License Number		
Man					Pastor		County		
					Date		State		
Woman					Place		License Number		
Man					Pastor		County		
					Date		State		
Woman					Place		License Number		

B-Baptized Member   P-Professing Member   AF-Affiliate Member   AS-Associate Member   CR-Constituency Roll

RECORD OF MARRIAGES

FULL NAME			ADDRESS	CHURCH RELATION-SHIP	OFFICIANT, DATE, AND PLACE OF MARRIAGE			LICENSE ISSUED BY			NEW ADDRESS
FAMILY	FIRST	MID-			Pastor	Date	Place	County	State	License Number	
Man											
Woman											
Man											
Woman											
Man											
Woman											
Man											
Woman											
Man											
Woman											
Man											
Woman											
Man											
Woman											
Man											
Woman											
Man											
Woman											

B-Baptized Member   P-Professing Member   AF-Affiliate Member   AS-Associate Member   CR-Constituency Roll

RECORD OF MARRIAGES

FAMILY	FULL NAME		ADDRESS	CHURCH RELATION-SHIP	OFFICIANT, DATE, AND PLACE OF MARRIAGE		LICENSE ISSUED BY		NEW ADDRESS
	FIRST	MID-							
Man					Pastor		County		
Woman					Date		State		
					Place		License Number		
Man					Pastor		County		
Woman					Date		State		
					Place		License Number		
Man					Pastor		County		
Woman					Date		State		
					Place		License Number		
Man					Pastor		County		
Woman					Date		State		
					Place		License Number		
Man					Pastor		County		
Woman					Date		State		
					Place		License Number		
Man					Pastor		County		
Woman					Date		State		
					Place		License Number		
Man					Pastor		County		
Woman					Date		State		
					Place		License Number		
Man					Pastor		County		
Woman					Date		State		
					Place		License Number		
Man					Pastor		County		
Woman					Date		State		
					Place		License Number		

B-Baptized Member   P-Professing Member   AF-Affiliate Member   AS-Associate Member   CR-Constituency Roll

89

RECORD OF DEATHS
(Recommended)

Use the chronological reference number in recording deaths. It would be helpful to list the membership of the deceased: Was he or she a professing member (P), baptized member (B), affiliate (AF) or associate (AS) member, or on the Constituency Roll (CR)? This record will provide a complete list of all funerals provided by the ministry of the church.

The provision for indicating church relationship will assist in identifying which deaths were those of members and which were nonmembers.

"Disposition of the Body" covers the option of burial, cremation, or other means.

The name of the officiant at the service should be included to show continuity of pastoral care within the church.

Prepared and edited by the General Council on Finance and Administration. Published by The United Methodist Publishing House, Nashville, Tennessee.

RECORD OF DEATHS

FULL NAME		CHURCH RELATION-SHIP	CHRONO-LOGICAL REFERENCE NUMBER	DATE OF DEATH	DISPOSITION OF BODY		OFFICIANT
FAMILY	FIRST	MID-				CEMETERY, CREMATION, OTHER	CITY, COUNTY, AND STATE	

P-Professing Member   B-Baptized Member   AF-Affiliate Member   AS-Associate Member   CR-on Constituency Roll

1

RECORD OF DEATHS

| FAMILY | FULL NAME | | CHURCH RELATON- SHIP | CHRONO- LOGICAL REFERENCE NUMBER | DATE OF DEATH | DISPOSITION OF BODY | | OFFICIANT |
	FIRST	MID-				CEMETERY, CREMATION, OTHER	CITY, COUNTY, AND STATE	

P-Professing Member   B-Baptized Member   AF-Affiliate Member   AS-Associate Member   CR-on Constituency Roll

RECORD OF DEATHS

| FULL NAME | | | CHURCH RELATION-SHIP | CHRONO-LOGICAL REFERENCE NUMBER | DATE OF DEATH | DISPOSITION OF BODY | | OFFICIANT |
FAMILY	FIRST	MID-				CEMETERY, CREMATION, OTHER	CITY, COUNTY, AND STATE	

P-Professing Member   B-Baptized Member   AF-Affiliate Member   AS-Associate Member   CR-on Constituency Roll

RECORD OF DEATHS

FAMILY	FULL NAME		CHURCH RELATION-SHIP	CHRONO-LOGICAL REFERENCE NUMBER	DATE OF DEATH	DISPOSITION OF BODY		OFFICIANT
	FIRST	MID-				CEMETERY, CREMATION, OTHER	CITY, COUNTY, AND STATE	

P-Professing Member   B-Baptized Member   AF-Affiliate Member   AS-Associate Member   CR-on Constituency Roll

RECORD OF DEATHS

FAMILY	FULL NAME		CHURCH RELATION-SHIP	CHRONO-LOGICAL REFERENCE NUMBER	DATE OF DEATH	DISPOSITION OF BODY		OFFICIANT
	FIRST	MID-				CEMETERY, CREMATION, OTHER	CITY, COUNTY, AND STATE	

P-Professing Member   B-Baptized Member   AF-Affiliate Member   AS-Associate Member   CR-on Constituency Roll

5

RECORD OF DEATHS

| FULL NAME | | | CHURCH RELATION-SHIP | CHRONO-LOGICAL REFERENCE NUMBER | DATE OF DEATH | DISPOSITION OF BODY | | OFFICIANT |
FAMILY	FIRST	MID-				CEMETERY, CREMATION, OTHER	CITY, COUNTY, AND STATE	

P-Professing Member   B-Baptized Member   AF-Affiliate Member   AS-Associate Member   CR-on Constituency Roll

CPSIA information can be obtained
at www.ICGtesting.com
Printed in the USA
LVHW062137200723
753039LV00007BA/23

9 780687 359134